COUNSELING AND DEVELOPMENT SERIES
ALLEN IVEY, *Editor*

The Construction and Understanding of Psychotherapeutic Change

CONVERSATIONS, MEMORIES, AND THEORIES

Jack Martin

Teachers College, Columbia University
New York and London

Published by Teachers College Press, 1234 Amsterdam Avenue,
New York, N.Y., 10027

Library of Congress Cataloging-in-Publication Data

Martin, Jack, 1950–
   The construction and understanding of psychotherapeutic change :
conversations, memories, and theories / Jack Martin.
      p.   cm. — (Counseling and development series)
   Includes bibliographical references and index.
   ISBN 0-8077-3337-7 (acid-free paper). — ISBN 0-8077-3336-9 (pbk.:
acid-free paper)
   1. Psychotherapy. 2. Personality change. 3. Autobiographical
memory. 4. Personal construct theory. 5. Conversations—
Psychological aspects. 6. Influence (Psychology)   I. Title.
II. Series.
RC480.5.M336   1994
   616.89′14′01—dc20   93-44505

ISBN 0-8077-3337-7
ISBN 0-8077-3336-9 (pbk.)

Printed on acid-free paper
Manufactured in the United States of America

01 00 99 98 97 96 95 94   8 7 6 5 4 3 2 1

CONTENTS

FOREWORD

How did I become the person I am? Why do I think, feel, and lead my life as I do? Finally, is there hope that I might alter the trajectory of my life to better achieve specific goals? I am certain you'll agree that these three questions touch on central issues for modern philosophy and psychology. While definitive answers to the questions now lie beyond our ken, Jack Martin suggests some promising leads as to where answers might lie. In response to these three questions, Martin directs our attention toward memories, theories, and conversations.

Martin sees action as foundational to human life. Beginning even before birth, a child interacts with whatever environments she or he makes contact. In these interactions, the child not only strives to understand the external world but also attempts to come to an understanding of him or herself. The salient memories of one's life serve as active, molding forces in the continued development of the person for many years after the events occur.

In time, each person develops a theory about him or herself. That is, a theory about our lives, our circumstances, and important others in our lives. These personal theories explain the developmental trajectories of our lives, describe how each of us became the person we are, and suggest our preference for certain possible futures over others. In short, the theory each of us holds about the meaning of life plays an active role in the creation of the life that each of us eventually lives. As active agents we are at least partially responsible (significant others, historical events, and autobiographical accidents also influence our life's trajectory) for the paths our lives travel.

Finally, in Martin's view, conversations are among the most important events in our lives. We can literally talk ourselves into our futures via private conversations (where I explain or think-through issues to myself), conversations with significant others such as family members and friends, and through overarching societal and cultural discussions. A form of conversation of special interest to psychologists is psychotherapy. Because Martin sees the development of the self as an evolving theory that emerges from memories of earlier, significant conversations, he is well-positioned to explain how the conversations a client carries on internally or with others can produce real change in her or his life. Therapeutic conversations set in motion changes in the trajectory of the client's life by altering the conversations a client carries on internally or with others in his or her life.

While *The Construction and Understanding of Psychotherapeutic Change* focuses on the psychotherapeutic conversation, it is quite different from most other books about psychotherapy. The emphasis of other books tends to be on prescriptive issues — how might a therapist go about conducting psychotherapy. Martin takes a completely different approach; his aim is to explicate a basic model of how it is that psychotherapy works when it works. Memories, theories, and conversations reciprocally interact with one another throughout our lives in complex ways to yield the person, situation, and problem that each client brings to therapy. A relationship develops between a client and therapist that spawns a very special type of conversation — a helping relationship wherein a therapeutic conversation will develop. The primary purpose of this therapeutic conversation is to enable the client to more effectively deal with the problems that brought him or her to therapy. But because his analysis deals with the basic conversational mechanisms of psychological change, Martin has chosen to offer few concrete hints in this book as to how a therapist ought to conduct psychotherapy.

Just as paradox and irony often emerge in therapy, Martin's book also produced a paradoxical impact on me. While he gave few concrete suggestions regarding how to conduct therapy, I felt that the book might change my approach in working with clients because it tempted me to modify my understanding of how therapeutic change occurs. Perhaps my experience is simply another data point to suggest the wisdom of the aphorism often attributed to Kurt Lewin that, "There is nothing so practical as a good theory." Because I saw so many practical applications to Martin's theoretical observations, I am tempted to claim that what he offers us is a very good theory indeed.

A word more needs to be added regarding the interdisciplinary style of Martin's scholarship. One's fundamental assumptions (regarding science, epistemology, human nature, etc.) will of necessity constrict what one can imagine about a topic like psychotherapy. Jack Martin feels that many of the earlier analyses of how psychotherapy works foundered upon the rocks of wrongheaded philosophical assumptions (e.g., dualism). Thus, the author goes to great lengths to articulate his vision of an adequate ontology of human nature (a nondualistic, agenic model) and his perspective on philosophy of science (a critical realist approach). In order to explicate this basic position, the reader is treated to a selective introduction to the research programs of some of the most important contemporary theoreticians in philosophy (e.g., Harré, Bhaskar, Rorty, Greenwood, Taylor) and psychology (e.g., Tulving, Paivio, Marcus, Mahoney, Beck). In the process, the reader begins to see science and human nature as Jack Martin sees them. With this empathic appreciation for the author's vision, the reinterpretation of psychotherapy—as a most important, change producing conversation embedded in a lifetime of other memories, personal theories, and conversations—becomes most plausible.

Martin's vision is distinctive, consistent with current theories and models of change in psychology, suggestive of new ways to approach the challenge of psychotherapy, and nicely corroborated by his own program of empirical research. The total package is well worth our time and consideration. It represents, in my judgment, a fine example of the cross-fertilization of science and practice. I trust you also will be challenged and edified by Martin's unique vision of the place of the therapeutic conversation in our clients' lives.

George S. Howard, Notre Dame, IN

PREFACE

Theories of psychotherapy have proliferated during the latter half of this century. Mostly, these theories attempt to describe *what* therapeutic ingredients are best suited to assisting clients to change. Questions about *how* psychotherapy works to effect client change typically receive scant attention in such prescriptive theories. When they are pursued, the theoretical bases for understanding *questions of how,* frequently are borrowed from theories of human development and learning extant in other areas of psychology and social science. For the most part, we know surprisingly little about how the psychotherapeutic conversations and activities engaged by therapists and their clients enable client change in extratherapeutic contexts.

In this book, I have attempted to provide a rather general theory of psychotherapeutic change that is intended to apply to most instances of psychotherapy with clients whose functioning is not severely disabled. The uniqueness of the view I present arises from my adoption of a social-cultural, as opposed to a biological, perspective. Yet, unlike some other attempts to locate the origins of human psychological processes in social-cultural practices, my approach does *not* deny the existence of psychological processes with real causal force. While maintaining that the psychological is constituted from the social, I hold that the psychological is not reducible to the social. More specifically, I claim that the psychological constructions of individuals originate in the forms and constructions of social conversation and practice, but are not entirely constrained by these conversations and practices. In particular, I maintain that one's memories of past experiences in conversations and social practices, are the bases for the personal theories that one holds about oneself, others, and one's life situations. Further, I hold that these memories and the personal theories they support can be altered by exposure to more recent, different conversational/practical experiences. Psychotherapy is a potentially powerful collection of conversations and practical activities capable of initiating changes to individuals' experiential memories and personal theories, changes that enable altered ways of acting in extratherapeutic contexts.

In developing my theory of how psychotherapy works to enable client change, I borrow from a variety of social-cultural and psychological perspectives on human conversation, memory, and theory construction, especially the construction of theories of "self." While all the perspectives from which I borrow are not naturally compatible, I attempt to meld what I take from them into a theory of psychotherapeutic change that is both internally cohesive and externally coherent. I also attempt to provide initial empirical support for aspects of my theory that are more contingent than analytic, support that derives from the intensive study of actual psychotherapy sessions. In the end, I think that the work I present provides a reasonable answer to a question that has intrigued me since I first studied psychological therapy as an undergraduate: How is it that conversations between psychotherapists and their clients might enable client change outside of psychotherapy? I only can hope that at least some readers might hold similar questions, and experience a similar sense of "having been informed."

I am indebted to many individuals who have contributed to this work in direct and indirect ways. My own memories of conversations with my friends, colleagues, and students undoubtedly form the basis for much of what I have included in these pages. In particular, I was helped by Jeff Sugarman and Judy Lapadat, both of whom read and commented on drafts of this work. Eileen Mallory assisted me in preparing the manuscript. Brian Ellerbeck of Teachers College Press provided solid support and insightful counsel throughout the entire process of writing this book. Allen Ivey, in his role as Series Editor, was largely responsible for giving me the opportunity to write the book in the first place.

In addition, the work presented herein would not have been possible without continuous support from the Social Sciences and Humanities Research Council of Canada (Grants #410-91-1740, #410-88-0022, #410-86-0225, and #410-84-0045). I also would like to thank The Guilford Press, Heldref Publications, and Lawrence Erlbaum Associates for permission to use and adapt small sections of previously published material. In chapter 1, I have used some material from my previously published article, "The Problem with Therapeutic Science," which appeared in *Journal of Psychology, 127,* pp. 365–374, published by Heldref Publications in 1993. In chapter 2, I have quoted and adapted material from a chapter by Laura Rice and Eva Saperia, "Task Analysis of the Resolution of Problematic Reactions," which appeared in Rice, L. N., and Greenberg, L. S. (Eds.) (1984). *Patterns of Change: Intensive Analysis of Psychotherapy Process.* New York: The Guilford Press. In chapter 3, I have borrowed and adapted brief sections from two other previously published articles of my own: (a) Martin, J. (1991). The Social-Cognitive Construction of Therapeutic Change: A Dual Coding Analysis. *Journal of Social and Clinical Psychology, 10,* 305–321 (a Guilford publication); and (b) Martin, J. (1993). Episodic Memory: A Neglected Phenomenon in the Psychology of Education. *Educational Psychologist, 28,* 169–183 (a Lawrence Erlbaum publication).

The Construction
and Understanding of
Psychotherapeutic Change

———————————

CONVERSATIONS, MEMORIES, AND THEORIES

Chapter 1

A TEMPLATE FOR HUMAN CHANGE

In their own private sphere, human beings retain the functions of social interaction. (Vygotsky, 1981, p. 164)

This book attempts an empirically supported, theoretical explanation of how humans might change as a consequence of their participation in psychological therapy. The explanation proposed is assumed to hold across different forms of psychotherapy directed at adults who are not seriously disturbed, but who voluntarily seek assistance in resolving or coping with problems they experience in their lives. Such difficulties might involve interpersonal conflicts, anxieties and stress, vocational and life-style decision-making, major and minor life transitions, existential ruminations and issues of identity, parenting and child rearing, death and loss, personal and professional development, and communication and relationship issues.

We humans are unique conversationalists, mnemonicists, and theoreticians. Throughout our lives, we participate in ongoing *conversations* with other people. Our conversations include both our verbal and nonverbal attempts to communicate, as well as those sets of practical activities that typically accompany our communicative attempts. Sometimes our participation is direct; sometimes it is indirect. Sometimes our conversations are with individuals we know personally; sometimes they are less intimate interactions within more anonymous societal and cultural groups. Through conversation, we construct, develop, and exchange understandings about our surroundings, other people, and our own experiences, beliefs, and values. Our *memories* of the conversations in which we participate enable us to appropriate such understandings into personal *theories* that we hold about ourselves, others, and our circumstances. These theories, in interaction with our current experiences, constitute a basis for our own actions, our own contributions to the conversations in which we are embedded. An ongoing cycle of taking from and contributing to personal, social, and cultural conversations is the essence of the human experience. Our own memories and theories are taken from conversations, and return to conversations. We do not exist apart from the social and cultural conversations in which we are embedded. We literally imbibe and express *ourselves* (our theories of self) from and through these conversations.

The foregoing template for human development and change is not unknown in Western psychology, but neither is it common. By refusing to make a sharp distinction between the social and the personal (the public and the private; the "outer" and the "inner"), this approach falls outside of the vast majority of psychological work in North America and Western Europe. Unlike the radical dualisms contained in most psychoanalytic, cognitive, and humanistic models of human learning and development, the inner world of the individual is not separated from the outer world of the social, cultural, and historical. Unlike the deterministic features of most behavioral, biological, and strictly sociological models of human learning and development, the memories and theories that individuals appropriate from the conversations in which they participate may enable them to "go beyond" past conversations, to contribute in potentially unique ways to current and future conversations. Thus, while the personal arises from the social, it is not necessarily isomorphic with it and may transcend it.

OVERVIEW OF TEXT

To hold that the personal arises from the social, but is not entirely determined by it, is a viewpoint that has developed outside of mainstream Western social science. Nonetheless, it is the position that I endorse, defend, and develop in this book. In so doing, I make no claim to a generally unique contribution, although some of the specific proposals I make may contain somewhat original features. Related perspectives have been developed historically by theorists as diverse as Janet (cf. Ellenberg, 1970), Mead (1934/1974), Ryle (1949), and, most notably, Vygotsky (1934/1986). More recently, such views have been elaborated and extended in important works by Greenwood (1989, 1991a, 1991b), Harré (1984), Taylor (1989), and Wertsch (1991), among others. Of course, as will become apparent in later discussions, these various views are not identical, nor is my own perspective compatible with all aspects of them. However, what is distinctly novel in the current volume is my attempt to provide and defend a theory of therapeutic change consistent with a social-cultural developmental perspective that still leaves room for the exercise of human agency. *Psychological therapy is a unique form of conversation that attempts to alter the personal theories about themselves, others, and their own life circumstances that clients have acquired through their participation in other (previous and ongoing) intimate, social, and cultural conversations.* My primary strategy in this volume is to integrate the work of Lev Vygotsky (1934/1986), Rom Harré (1984), and Charles Taylor (1989) with the psychological theories of memory proposed by Alan Paivio (1986) and Endel Tulving (1983, 1985) and the psychology of personal theories developed by George Kelly (1955) and others. The result is a theoretical model that has been tested and elaborated through my own, and other, ongoing programs of research on psychotherapeutic change.

What I hope to show convincingly is that clients' memories for particular conversational episodes and content taken from psychological therapy mediate between experiences in therapy and functional alterations to clients' theories of themselves and their circumstances. It is these theoretical revisions that enable actions and experiences previously unavailable to clients. Through such changes, clients are able to overcome or cope more successfully with the problems that caused them to seek psychological therapy.

I begin by articulating a philosophical position capable of supporting the model of therapeutic change I just have sketched. This position is an adaptation, for my purposes, of a recently articulated philosophy of social and human science that has come to be called *critical realism* (cf. Bhaskar, 1989; Greenwood, 1991a; Harré, 1984; Manicas & Secord, 1983). Critical realism, as I will employ it, offers a relatively nondualistic, nonrelativistic basis for a historical, cultural account of human actions and psychological states. Within this account, human actions and psychological states are socially located and both collectively and individually represented. Humans construct theories of themselves, others, and their circumstances on the basis of their social, cultural, and linguistic histories. Thus, human constructivism is constrained in that the origins of human constructions are believed to lie in real social-cultural forms and practices. Nonetheless, the personal memories and theories that arise from this social-cultural background are not fully determined by the "background." The unique capability of humans to exercise some degree of agency and self-determination follows from the underdetermination of personal theories by direct personal experiences in social-cultural contexts. Humans are intentional agents capable of adapting their socially spawned theories and actions to their purposes and goals. This position and its implications for the study of therapeutic change are elaborated in the remainder of this introductory chapter.

Following this chapter are three chapters (chapters 2, 3, and 4), each of which discusses theoretical and empirical considerations related to human *conversations, memories,* and *theories,* respectively. As already summarized, the primary template for therapeutic change that I endorse involves an appropriation of elements from therapeutic conversations and interactions into clients' personal theories of themselves and their circumstances. This appropriation (or internalization) is brought about through the mediation of clients' memories of therapeutic conversations and their content. Consequently, a detailed treatment of each of the major components in this template is warranted. Each of the next three chapters begins with a brief overview of central issues, followed by a discussion of the seminal work of major contributors—Vygotsky, Harré, and Taylor with respect to *conversations,* Tulving and Paivio with respect to *memories,* and Kelly, Harré, Taylor, and Markus with respect to *personal theories.* These initial discussions are followed by a detailed presentation of my theory of psychotherapeutic change, a presentation that becomes increasingly complete as the reader moves through chapters 2, 3, and 4. Finally, each of these chapters concludes with a summation of supporting empirical and theoretical work conducted by myself, my immediate colleagues, and others. Considered together, these chapters hopefully will enable a clear, reasonably complete understanding of how human memories mediate between the conversations that constitute therapeutic interventions and resultant changes to clients' theories and actions.

The final chapter of the book (chapter 5) presents a formal summary of the core propositions and corollaries that constitute the theory of therapeutic change that has been presented. Implications of the theory for the practice of psychotherapy, the education of psychotherapists, and the conduct of research on psychotherapy then are examined.

A CRITICAL REALIST FOUNDATION

Much of the support for the theory of therapeutic change that I develop in this book derives from theory-testing, empirical research. Therefore, it is important to clarify the ontological and epistemological commitments that I believe define the relationship between psychological theories of this type and their empirical support. These commitments might best be described as generally consistent with what recently has become known as the *critical realist* position in the philosophy of social science, especially as advanced by Bhaskar (1989), Greenwood (1991a, 1991b), and Harré (1984) with respect to social psychological science. This position attempts to establish the ontological status of human actions and experiences (psychological states) as a precondition for psychological inquiry. Questions of epistemology (e.g., "How is psychological knowledge possible?") are pursued only once ontological, prior questions (e.g., "What are the phenomena of psychology?") have been addressed. In the following section, I provide a brief introduction to the ontological and epistemological views associated with my own version of critical realism. I then endeavor to show how these views might support psychological inquiry based on the template for human change I endorse in this book. In so doing, I offer a defense of the specific methods of theory construction and empirical testing I have used to develop the theory of therapeutic change that I present in the rest of this volume.

Ontological Status of Human Actions and Experiences

Human actions and psychological states are the basic objects of psychological science. Unlike the objects of study in natural science, neither human actions nor experiences are constituted atomistically. Neither can be decomposed into subcomponents that constitute their essential makeup, as, for example, water can be decomposed into molecules consisting of hydrogen and oxygen atoms. Rather than being atomistically constituted, human actions and psychological states are both socially located and represented in the collective and individual understandings of actors and those who witness human actions. For example, the humiliation I suffered as a young child upon failing my "tadpole" swimming lessons is defined by my presence at a public awards ceremony during which I stood with others, many of whom were called forward to receive their certificates of accomplishment, while my name remained uncalled throughout the entire ceremony. The presence of my parents and friends, the former at my request, and my lack of prior knowledge about my failure were important social and private elements in my humiliation.

Before it is possible to study psychological phenomena, it is necessary to arrive at a clear conception of the social and representational elements that define these phenomena. What is required is *not* an operational definition in which the phenomena of interest are equated with elements in their physical display, but a conceptual model that captures the critical social locations and personal/collective representations of these focal phenomena. For example, human humiliation cannot be equated with some set of "observables" alone, nor can it be conceptualized adequately by ignoring its appropriate social context. What is needed is a clear set of defining statements that capture both its social and representational aspects. Important elements in the former likely would include the public nature of the relevant events, together with some establishment of intimate (or, at least, meaningful) relations among the individual suffering humiliation and some of those who observe the events in question. Additionally, at a representational level, the humiliated individual must be known to care about these events (to attach some importance to them, perhaps in association with some cherished identity project), and those observing the events also must imbue them with some importance, either deriving from their knowledge of the suffering individual or their own values and beliefs.

It probably is one of the great tragedies of psychological science (cf. Danziger, 1990) that detailed ontological conceptualizations of focal phenomena are seldom undertaken prior to the commencement of empirical and theoretical study of these phenomena. Operationalism of the sort associated with naive empiricism in psychological science is no substitute for adequate conceptual framing of human actions and psychological states.

The fact that the objects of psychological science are socially located and collectively/personally represented does *not* mean that they are not real and cannot be studied with some accepted degree of scientific objectivity. Just because psychological phenomena are nonatomistic and defined in terms of their social locations and representations does not mean that they can be construed in any manner whatsoever. The social construction of psychological phenomena does not lead to relativism in their study. Conceptualizations of phenomena such as human humiliation are grounded in social, cultural, linguistic, and historical conventions. While it is true that such conventions may change over time and across societies/cultures, humans (including human/psychological scientists) are socialized into the norms, understandings, and conventions of their societies. The products of such socialization are not especially ephemeral. It is within these conventions that conceptualizations of psychological phenomena are constructed. Both societal conventions and social scientists' conceptualizations are *real*. In social and psychological science, both the objects of inquiry and the conceptualizations (models, theories) that guide inquiry, and are tested through inquiry, are real entities, by virtue of the causal force they can exert on each other. For example, in our linguistic culture, we probably perceive certain actions and associated contexts as instances of "help-giving" because we have internalized some prototypic understanding of the concept of helping and are able to extend this conceptual understanding to actions and contexts that bear a *family resemblance* to it. It is not the case that we could, without extensive social/cultural engineering of a most unlikely sort, construct and use different conceptual models of helping or humiliation and still retain sensibility in our theories of such phenomena.

As made clear by Bhaskar (1989), "science employs two criteria for the ascription of reality to a posited object: a perceptual and a causal one" (p. 69). Because psychological phenomena (human actions and psychological states), when conceptualized adequately, inevitably include unobservable, imperceptible elements and relations, that does not mean they are not real. The causal criterion for reality works in psychological science just as it works in natural science for phenomena such as gravitational or magnetic fields.

The critical realist approach to the ontology of psychological phenomena eschews both positivistic criteria for reality in terms of operational definitions, and relativistic ontologies that would deny the reality of psychological phenomena. In critical realism, social constitutionism (the belief that the psychological arises from the social-cultural) is married to a form of ontological realism (the belief that both the social and the psychological are real).

Epistemological Status of Psychological Science

The ontological status of the objects of psychological science (i.e., human actions and experiences), as distinctive from the atomistically constituted objects of natural science, means that the same methodologies that have been employed to good effect in the natural sciences *cannot* be expected to work with the same effectiveness in the social and psychological sciences. Nonetheless, the ontological status of human actions and psychological states as real does mean that they can be studied scientifically, even objectively, within specified social, linguistic, cultural, and historical contexts.

The standard methodology in natural science is to isolate focal phenomena for study in unnatural, idealized contexts so that their quintessential causal properties can be discovered. Because such phenomena are atomistically constituted, their essence is not altered by such isolation (in specialized laboratories), but is given ideal circumstances in which to manifest its properties. Thus, for example, Galileo (cf. Chalmers, 1990) used idealized situations (frictionless pivots, perfect spheres rolling down perfectly flat, frictionless inclined planes, and the like) to establish his laws of motion, knowing full well that similar experiments conducted outside of these idealized situations would "fail." The causal laws established in physics, chemistry, and other natural sciences do not manifest themselves as empirical invariances under normal conditions. It is only under specialized laboratory contexts (with the seeming exception of astronomy) that such causal regularities are observable. When natural scientists move from the closed systems of idealized, laboratory settings to open, real-world systems, their causal laws suffer suppression and interference through interaction with other, unknown and unpredictable laws and regularities. Thus, it is hardly surprising that enormous amounts of knowledge in physics do not permit accurate predictions of earthquakes, weather patterns, or the movements of individual leaves in windstorms. The key to the success of physical science methodology is not empirical regularity under normal conditions. Rather, it is the development and empirical testing of theoretical models that include real, yet unobservable, causal mechanisms under idealized situations.

Unfortunately, the ontological status of human actions and experiences, such as those that constitute psychological therapy, makes them impossible to study under highly specialized laboratory or analogue settings. Once again, unlike physical phenomena, psychological phenomena are not constituted atomistically, but derive from their social locations and representations in collective and personal theories. When human actions and psychological states are isolated for study in specialized settings, they inevitably are *altered,* with the consequence that what is studied is not the same as what would be studied in normal social situations. Psychological scientists cannot succeed in studying something like humiliation or therapeutic change, as conceptualized herein, by subjecting participants in research to standardized scenarios and response formats. When these scenarios and formats are not part of actual identity projects of participating individuals, the personal significance of such experiences, an important conceptual element in what it means to experience humiliation or significant personal change, inevitably is absent. The critical point is that psychological phenomena exist in real-world, *open* systems and cannot exist in detached, *closed* systems.

Unfortunately, just as it is in natural science, it is difficult to discover causal laws in social science, laws that can be warranted through predictions about the phenomena in question in real-world, open systems. Consequently, the reason that natural science methodologies of isolation and discovery cannot be employed in social, psychological science (including therapeutic science) is not because the phenomena of social, psychological science are any less real or lawful than are their natural science counterparts. Rather, it is because social, psychological phenomena exist only in real-world, open systems within social, linguistic, cultural, and historical contexts. The fundamental epistemological, methodological conundrum facing psychological scientists, especially those working in applied contexts such as the study of psychotherapy, is that *they cannot conduct valid studies of focal phenomena in isolation from the real-world contexts of these phenomena, and yet the inevitable "causal noise" in any such open system makes the discovery and/or verification of causal relations in these contexts extremely difficult.* One possible approach to this difficulty, the one I have adopted in the work reported herein, is described next.

A Critical Realist Strategy for the Conduct of Psychological Inquiry

Implications of a critical realist ontology and epistemology for the conduct of psychological science relate to (1) the importance of conceptual frameworks and theoretical models, (2) the settings in which inquiry is conducted, (3) the nature of empirical tests, (4) the warrants of justification that might be employed to evaluate empirical tests of theoretical propositions, and (5) the structure of research programs.

Conceptual/theoretical framework. Given that human actions and psychological states are subject to social construction, but are nonetheless real and somewhat enduring entities, it is critical that inquiry begin with as full a conceptualization of the objects of study as possible. Conceptualization of the phenomena of interest initially should be based on extant promising theory and research concerning these phenomena and generally should be consistent with ordinary-language descriptions of these phenomena within the social/cultural contexts in which the psychological investigation is being conducted. Special attention should be given to the social locations and personal/collective representations that define focal phenomena. As early into a research program as possible, a theoretical model should be developed that attempts to explain important aspects of how the focal phenomena function (i.e., how they enter into hypothesized explanatory and causal relationships with other phenomena of interest, as determined by questions and purposes guiding the research program). Such models or theories should not consist of empirical statements of observable regularities, but should contain important propositions concerning underlying causal-explanatory mechanisms. Thought should be given to how data can be obtained that might test the causal-explanatory mechanisms postulated. Initial work in a research program may need to be quite exploratory. However, the purpose of this exploratory work should be to arrive at a more adequate conceptualization and modeling of focal phenomena and functional mechanisms, not simply to accumulate descriptive data consisting of observable regularities and probabilities. The purpose of empirical work is to build and test theory, not to accumulate data per se.

Setting. Not surprisingly, given the social location and personal/ collective representation of human actions and psychological states, psychological research programs should study phenomena of interest in the real-world settings in which they occur. For example, it simply is not possible to study therapeutic change outside of therapeutic and related extratherapeutic settings in which such change occurs. Since attempts to study human actions and psychological states in specialized laboratory or analogue settings inevitably court distortion of these phenomena, there really is no alternative if the critical realist emphasis on the primacy of the ontological status of objects of study is to be maintained. Consequently, the causal and explanatory mechanisms postulated in conceptual frameworks and theoretical models never will be subject to testing through the observance of entirely predictive, empirical regularities. Such displays are inevitably unavailable in real-world settings, even if the causal-explanatory propositions and mechanisms postulated are entirely lawful and regular. Other laws and mechanisms affecting focal and other phenomena in real-world settings make definitive empirical tests impossible in psychological science. However, the use of real-world settings does not mean that theories (emergent and developed) cannot be tested (supported or not supported).

The nature of empirical tests. Tests of theories must involve the interpretation of occurrences that are not entailed by the theories themselves. The explanatory-causal mechanisms contained in psychological theories likely will not themselves be observable, but their causal effects should be (if not perfectly, at least perceptibly). A major epistemological problem in much existing psychological research is that an unwarranted reliance on operational (as opposed to conceptual) definitions of focal phenomena has resulted in confusion over the desired relationship between theory and empirical observation. If phenomena and causal and explanatory mechanisms of interest are defined solely in terms of their observable regularities, observance of such regularities cannot constitute a satisfactory test of the theoretical propositions posited. This is so because such regularities are mostly isomorphic with (entirely entailed by) the operational descriptions that constitute the theory. Thus, much psychological research that has employed an operational strategy may be seen as attempting unnecessary empirical tests of analytic propositions.

The data become redundant because the propositions supposedly tested actually are true by logical, operational definition or by strong structural implication (cf. Greenwood, 1991a; Smedslund, 1979).

To avoid such problems, it is important that the theoretical models tested in psychological research consist, at least in part, of postulated causal-explanatory mechanisms not reducible to observable regularities per se. These underlying explanatory mechanisms ideally will be consistent with certain results of appropriate empirical tests, but not with other results that might conceivably be obtained in such tests. For example, if therapeutic change occurs through the mediation of clients' memories of particular conversational episodes, as I believe, tests of this proposition might be constructed in terms of empirically verifiable patterns of relationships among clients' stated recollections of therapy, recordings of actual therapeutic conversations, and records of clients' understandings of these and related, extratherapeutic experiences. None of these data ultimately are directly reducible to the personal memories, theories, and changes postulated in the theory of psychotherapeutic change being tested. However, tests can be constructed, such that in given situations and contexts, certain patterns of relationship may be seen to support the basic theoretical premises, while other possible patterns of results may be seen to cast doubt on their validity. Of course, given the nature of open systems, such as therapy sessions and related extratherapeutic contexts, no such tests ever will prove definitive, nor will extremely accurate predictions of specific results be possible. Nonetheless, the accumulation of supportive versus unsupportive tests over several studies within a research program, and across different research programs, may be seen to constitute a legitimate form of theory testing in psychological, therapeutic science.

Warrants of justification. What then enables psychological researchers to interpret the results of empirical tests of their theoretical propositions as supportive or unsupportive of these propositions? From a critical realist perspective, this question becomes, "What are defensible, useful warrants for psychological research in open systems?" If causal laws are thought to consist or manifest only as invariant empirical regularities, and if the point of psychological science is to establish such regularities (thus verifying operational theories), there would seem to be little hope of warranting psychological theories through empirical tests in open, real-world systems. Consequently, positivistic approaches to psychological inquiry become ensnared in intractable difficulties.

Hermeneutic or interpretive approaches to psychological inquiry (e.g., Hiley, Bohman, & Shusterman, 1991) attempt to address such difficulties by eschewing the notion that the aim of psychological inquiry is to establish causal explanations. Advocates of these approaches hold that appropriate interpretation of focal psychological phenomena is a more reasonable general objective. In the hermeneutic option, the building of theory occurs largely in a post hoc fashion and often is subservient to the goal of acquiring a kind of practical wisdom that results from placing psychological practice at the very center of inquiry (cf. Rorty, 1991b). While it is arguable, I believe that such hermeneutic inquiries tend to underestimate the difficulties of interpretation without at least some form of causal explanation. It is extremely difficult for me to imagine an explication of psychological phenomena that is entirely devoid of elements of enabling causality. Indeed, few reports of descriptive, interpretive research manage to avoid some (perhaps unintended, but probably necessary) ascription of causality in the clarifications they attempt (see Greenwood, 1989 and 1991b, for an extended discussion of relevant issues relating to description and explanation in social science). Thus, critical realism is somewhat unique in its attempt to explain psychological phenomena in terms of testable, causal propositions in real-world, open systems. Like hermeneutics, critical realism embraces human agency and the "contextualized" meaningfulness of human actions. Unlike most contemporary hermeneutic approaches, critical realism treats human reasons, beliefs, and understandings (in context) as possible enabling causes of actions.

What warrants of justification does critical realism endorse that permit the interpretation of empirical data as tests of causal explanations derivative from nonoperational, explanatory theories? The essential criteria I have adopted in my program of research on therapeutic change are *heuristic fertility* and *semipredictive utility*. The former derives from a joint focus on the *internal cohesion* and *external coherence* of the theory I have attempted to generate, develop, and test. The latter derives from my attempt to achieve some measure of *experimental closure* in the largely uncontrollable, unpredictive therapeutic settings in which my research program has been conducted.

Heuristic fertility refers to the ability of a psychological theory to generate significant hypotheses for empirical testing. In addition to an adequate conceptualization of focal phenomena, the significance of such hypotheses derives from the theory's internal cohesion and external coherence. The former requires that the interpretation of empirical data be consistent with the major theoretical propositions reflected in the hypotheses being tested. While no grounds exist for nonproblematic verification or refutation of hypotheses and theoretical propositions (cf. Phillips, 1987), empirical tests must be designed and interpreted in ways that confront central theoretical tenets with data relevant to their existence. Through such tests, the theory must evolve in ways that keep it from becoming self-contradictory, yet open to further empirical testing.

At the same time, the requirement of external coherence with respect to heuristic fertility means that the theory being developed and elaborated through empirical testing must maintain contact with other theoretical and empirical work that is related to the theory. This requirement does not mean that the theory must be entirely consistent with work outside of its immediate purview. However, if the theory is to avoid becoming entirely local, it must make contact with relevant extant work. Where such work can be interpreted to augment and support the theory under construction, the advantages gained by cross-theoretical contact are obvious. Where other work seems to contradict the theory being developed, such seeming contradictions sometimes might be accommodated by changes in the theory that do not threaten its internal cohesion, yet enhance its external coherence. At other times, empirical tests might be constructed and undertaken to attempt to support one or another of the competing possibilities. The warrant of heuristic fertility, and the subwarrants of internal cohesion and external coherence, help to ensure that psychological theories will be ideationally rich and nonlocal, but not at the cost of becoming untestable and all encompassing.

The second major warrant I endorse in the version of critical realism I have developed with respect to applied psychological theory (in this case, research on psychotherapeutic change) is semipredictive utility. Because psychological phenomena in real-world, open systems are largely unpredictive, and causal relationships are frequently obscured, that does not mean empirical tests cannot be constructed in such settings that will support or not support particular theoretical propositions. Interpretation of empirical results in open systems does not need to be entirely post hoc, and explanations for such results do not need to eschew causal forms. What is required is that some measure of naturally occurring or experimental *closure* be located or introduced in the conduct of real-world empirical tests. Such closures (i.e., naturally occurring or experimenter-manipulated situations in which interference conditions are relatively minimized) permit the researcher to predict at least some general patterns of results that can be interpreted as support for one or another predetermined theoretical hypotheses. When discussing specific studies conducted in support of the various theoretical propositions that constitute my theory of therapeutic change, I will provide several examples of such features. Some will involve the location of naturally occurring "control" events against which to compare therapeutic events of focal interest. Others will involve purposeful manipulations of therapeutic in-

terventions that are within the usual therapeutic repertoires of the therapists who offer them. Such closure features are absolutely critical to the
conduct of psychological research in otherwise open therapeutic systems
that aims at the production and testing of theoretical models that include
causal-explanatory mechanisms (see Greenwood, 1989).

The nature of psychological research programs. No single study,
or even group of studies, can be definitive with respect to testing psychological theories. The idea of the *research program* is of fundamental
importance in the development and testing of psychological theory. Critical realist accounts of research programs in the social sciences emphasize
their cyclical, tripartite nature.

> So we have in science a three-phase schema of development, in which
> in a continuing dialectic, science identifies a phenomenon (or range of
> phenomena), constructs explanations for it and empirically tests its
> explanations, leading to the identification of the generative mechanism
> at work, which now becomes the phenomenon to be explained, and so
> on. (Bhaskar, 1989, pp. 68–69)

It is important to note that this view of scientific research programs
construes the essence of science to lie in a transition from the study of
manifest phenomena to the study of underlying structures thought to
generate such observables. This fundamental idea is believed to hold
across both natural and social science, subject to the important differences noted earlier in the nature of social psychological versus natural
phenomena.

My own research program has attempted to articulate as fully as
possible essential phenomena and propositions in the basic template for
human change summarized at the beginning of this chapter. To this end,
I have been assisted by the seminal work of individuals such as Vygotsky,
Harré, Taylor, Paivio, Tulving, Kelly, and Markus. I have attempted to
articulate conceptual models of change processes and mechanisms in
therapeutic contexts. Sometimes, preliminary, exploratory inquiries have
been necessary to assist the formulation of these models. However, the
primary empirical work I have engaged has attempted to test central
propositions in these models against displays of relevant data that can
be construed to support, or not to support, them or their competitors
(when such have been available). With the conduct of each successive
study, I have been able to obtain slightly greater degrees of experimental
control over conditions likely to affect the phenomena of central interest,
and to posit more complete and more elegant descriptions of relevant

causal and explanatory mechanisms. Through a combination of attention to both internal cohesion and external coherence, I have attempted to provide an elaborated theory of human change in therapeutic contexts that is consistent with the basic template articulated at the outset of this chapter — that is, that significant human change in such settings involves alterations to the personal theories of participants that are enabled through the memory-mediated appropriation of therapeutic conversations. It is this theoretical and conceptual work that I will describe in the remainder of this volume.

Chapter 2

CONVERSATIONS

The primary human reality is persons in conversations.
(R. Harré, 1984, p. 58)

Therapeutic conversations are the verbal and nonverbal exchanges and activities that occur between therapists and clients during the course of psychotherapy. Conversations between psychotherapists and clients minimally constitute psychological therapy. Frank (1974) has suggested that the feature common to all successful counseling and psychotherapy is the ability to interact with a trusted and respected person in a course of activities that both believe may produce a therapeutic change. This simple social, descriptive characterization of psychological therapy may be transformed into a theoretical, causal-explanatory claim: that the efficacy of all therapies (psychoanalytic, experiential, behavioral, cognitive, systemic, and others) may simply be a product of the type of interaction described by Frank under the conditions of "shared belief" specified in his description (cf. Greenwood, 1991a, p. 130). The belief that such a minimal explanation is sufficient to explain therapeutic change separates social psychological from cognitive psychological and experiential/humanistic theorizing about therapeutic change.

Many influential social psychological theories of therapeutic change (e.g., Jackson, 1961; Kiesler, 1982; Strong & Claiborn, 1982) emphasize social interactions between therapists and clients during psychotherapy, viewing change as a process of interpersonal influence. Some (e.g., Claiborn, 1988; Heesacker, 1986) have added a definite cognitive component to such social psychological theories by incorporating models of attitude change and cognitive restructuring into their descriptive and explanatory frameworks. Nonetheless, the social psychological approach

16

to the study of therapeutic change remains wedded to change mechanisms that are located in the social interactions of psychotherapy (cf. Strong, Welsh, Corcoran, & Hoyt, 1992).

Contemporary cognitive and experiential theories of therapeutic change emphasize hypothetical change mechanisms that affect clients' mental (cognitive, perceptual, and affective) representations and organizations. Such mechanisms are said to occasion alterations and revisions to clients' personal theories or belief systems about themselves, others, and their own experiences (cf. Dryden & Golden, 1986; Mahoney & Freeman, 1985). In these theories, the minimal explanation of therapeutic change as social influence is replaced by more metaphysical speculations about mental and experiential change processes that underlie clients' actions.

For the most part, social psychological and cognitive psychological theories of therapeutic change have been developed apart from each other. Extensive work has been done on both sides of the social–cognitive bridge, but little work has focused specifically on the bridge itself.

Theoretical distance between social and cognitive/experiential accounts of therapeutic change is not surprising given that most Western psychology continues to unfold in the traditions of Freud and Piaget (cf. Danziger, 1990). Both Freudian and Piagetian perspectives are radically dualistic. Both view human mental and intellectual accomplishments as mediated by sustained social pressures. In both theoretical frameworks, it is assumed that the individual already possesses some (perhaps initially primitive, irrational, or syncretic) forms of thought, or potential thought, by virtue of biological factors. This assumption casts development as a lifelong adaptation of the internal/private to the external/social. In Piaget's (1969) words:

> The psychology of thought is always faced at this point with two fundamental factors, whose connection it is her task to explain: the biological factor, and the social factor. We have here two different planes, theoretically independent of one another, and which logically one would wish to keep separate: but in practice, these two planes will always be associated, so long as the child has parents who represent Society to him, and as long as he experiences sensations which constitute a biological environment. (p. 201)

Piaget's work, like that of Freud before him, is permeated with the idea of the gradual socialization of biologically determined structures and functions of thought.

THE VYGOTSKIAN ALTERNATIVE

Traditional Western dualism (i.e., the conservation of theoretical and/or functional independence of the social and the biological, or the social and the cognitive/experiential), as enshrined in the works of Freud, Piaget, and their followers, is attacked relentlessly in the work of Lev Vygotsky (1934/1986). For Vygotsky, the earliest speech of the child already is social. Both speech and thought are fundamentally a product of social reality, not of biology as mediated by social factors.

> If we were to summarize the central flaws in Piaget's theory, we would have to point out that it is reality and the relations between a child and reality that are missed in his theory. The process of socialization appears as a direct communication of souls, which is divorced from the practical activity of a child. (pp. 51–52)

Vygotsky's central point is that participation in social life and conversations is a form of practical activity that gives meaning to the words and concepts employed, some of which is appropriated (*internalized*) by individual actors/conversationalists as a basis for inner speech and thought (which is distinguishable from inner speech). Without such internalization, there is no inner speech or thought, just a set of primitive, natural, mental functions (elementary perception, memory, and attention) that enable largely independent forms of preintellectual speech and preverbal thought. Thus, Vygotsky attempts to explain how individual thoughts and theories arise from the social, not how biologically determined, individual tendencies are socialized.

Vygotsky insists that the earliest speech of the child is social. In early childhood (roughly ages 3 to 7), the child's original social speech divides into egocentric and communicative speech. The former is speech for oneself. The latter is speech for others. It is egocentric speech, extracted from general social speech, that gives rise to inner speech or individualized verbal thought. However, it is not the appropriation of egocentric speech into individualized thought that, by itself, constitutes a sufficient basis for thought. Egocentric speech serves as a model for verbal thought, but it does not provide rich content for such thought. The major problem for Vygotsky was to explain how communicative speech for and from others becomes individualized as thought. To do so, he theorized that outward, *inter*psychological relations become the inner, *intra*psychological mental functions. Through the child's indirect and direct participation in intimate, social, and cultural conversations, culturally sanctioned, symbolic systems become remodeled into individual verbal thought. Overt dialogue is internalized as internal dialogue.

However, it is important to note that Vygotsky, while viewing thought and speech as overlapping in verbal thought, did not view thought and speech as isomorphic. Verbal thought does not by any means include all forms of thought or all forms of speech. Much in thought may be socially mediated, yet nonverbal. Vygotsky also tended to view verbal thought (inner speech) as much more than an internal aspect of talking.

> In inner speech two important processes are interwoven: the transition from external communication to inner dialogue and the expression of intimate thoughts in linguistic form, thus making them communicative. Inner speech becomes a psychological interface between, on the one hand, culturally sanctioned symbolic systems and, on the other hand, private "language" and imagery. The concretization of psychological activity in this context appears as a psychological mechanism for creating new symbols and word senses capable of eventually being incorporated into the cultural stock. (Kozulin, 1986, p. xxxviii)

In Vygotsky's work, the focus is on the interrelations and interfunctions of the social (conversations and practical activity) and the cognitive/experiential (higher mental functions, knowledge, beliefs, and personal theories). To continue an earlier metaphor, Vygotsky focuses on the bridge, the connection between the personal and the social, not on the sides it connects. The radical dualism of Piaget and Freud is replaced by a cultural, historical perspective in which the private (cognitive) arises from the public (social), retains ongoing kinship (although not isomorphism) with public forms and functions, and eventually may come to exert a somewhat creative influence on these public phenomena. The recent work of Rom Harré (1984) extends and elaborates this basic Vygotskian developmental perspective.

Harré's Extension of Vygotsky's Developmental Sequence

Harré's (1984) neo-Vygotskian theory of the development of persons encompasses four stages: (1) appropriation, (2) transformation, (3) publication, and (4) conventionalization. [My interpretations of Harré's developmental stages owe much to Sugarman (1992).] *Appropriation* is the process of internalization described by Vygotsky (1934/1986) through which publicly displayed, social, relational, and linguistic forms resident in public conversations and practical activities become reflected in the private, mental world of the developing individual. (Readers should note that future use in this volume of the term *conversation* is intended to connote both conversation itself and the practical activities that accompany it.) Such internalized conceptual and linguistic forms then can be used as psychological tools through which the individual can enter the developmental stage of *transformation*. Transformation refers to the use of such psychological tools to organize an individual's ongoing experiences. During transformation, the very nature of an individual's experience in the world becomes altered. Whereas previously (i.e., during appropriation) the developing individual was internalizing forms from public conversations and activities, the individual now uses these internalized forms to begin to structure her or his own experiences. Particular events are instantiated with one's own private forms of experientially based understanding, thus enabling a distinctive, autobiographical, self-conscious sense to one's experiences in the world. Transformation thus culminates in the ordering of experiences as one's own.

Through the private display and realization of self-ascription that come with transformation, the individual becomes capable of *publication*. Publication involves the expression of the products of an individual's unique transformational processes in the public, social arena where they are exposed to the scrutiny of others. Publication is the transmitting to others of that which has been organized according to one's own transformational activities, according to one's developing theory of self. Finally, the stage of *conventionalization* unfolds during which the publicly displayed, individually realized psychological phenomena developed during the preceding stages become accepted into the shared knowledge and conventions of one's culture. Conventionalization involves the collective realization, sanctioning, and adoption of an individual's idiosyncratic constructions as part of the shared cultural milieu.

The significance of Harré's elaboration and extension of Vygotsky's developmental theory is that it enables a relatively nondualistic understanding of how an individual can both be a product of the societal, cultural conversations into which the individual was born and raised, and yet eventually come to be a creative contributor to those same conversations. For most of us, our agenic contributions are confined to the stories and collective memories that constitute the more narrow cultural histories of our families and local communities. However, some few of us succeed in contributing more widely to the broader societies and cultures to which we belong, perhaps through such creative acts as popular musical composition, publication of influential writings, actions of particular social significance, and the like. Harré's neo-Vygotskian theory of personal development and being is a detailed explication of the processes and mechanisms through which individuals imbibe public, social conversations; use the products of such appropriations as psychological tools to fashion their own experiences and theories of self; and ultimately contribute back to the social, cultural conversations in which they are embedded through unique expressions of their own individuality in the public arena. Of particular importance for a less dualistic, critical realist account of human change, such a developmental sequence relegates to the status of mythology conceptions of atomistic, disengaged individualism of the sort promulgated in much Western psychology and social science.

Taylor's Dialogical Perspective

Taking his lead from the neo-Vygotskian literary hermeneuticist, M. M. Bakhtin, Charles Taylor (1991) argues that

> Human beings are constituted in conversation; and hence what gets internalized in the mature subject is not [only] the reaction of the other, but the whole conversation, with the interanimation of its voices. Only a theory of this kind can do justice to the dialogical nature of the self. (p. 314)

In this, and many other passages (1989, 1991) Taylor assumes an important distinction between *monological* and *dialogical* acts. Taylor argues that it is impossible to understand human life only in terms of individual subjects who frame representations about and respond to others. Our identities are not defined adequately in terms of our individual properties. What is required is a full appreciation of how we come to incorporate entire dialogues, both practical and linguistic, into our understandings and actions.

To understand Taylor's conception of dialogical acts, it is necessary to grasp his views of "the body" and "the other." Following Heidegger (1962), Merleau-Ponty (1945), and Wittgenstein (1953), Taylor believes that much of our intelligent action in the world depends on an understanding that is largely inarticulate. This kind of understanding is "embodied." It is found in our nonverbalizable sense of socially appropriate manner, our implicit recognition of aesthetic form, and our practical knowledge of how to perform a range of activities from typing manuscripts to driving automobiles.

The origins of our embodied, practical know-how (as well as our more consciously accessible, verbalizable knowledge) are to be found in the dialogical forms and practices we internalize by virtue of our own direct and vicarious conversational experiences. For Taylor (and for

Bakhtin, 1986), conversations encompass the verbal and nonverbal actions of all conversational participants and include the practical accompaniments and functions of these actions. Thus, when we internalize conversations, in the Vygotskian sense, we appropriate the entire dialogue – the communications, the voices, the conversational context, and the practical consequences we witness. As a result, the understandings we develop based on our conversational inheritance are not restricted to our own monological activities and to those of an introjected other (as in Freud or perhaps even Mead), but include "self-generated transformations of the offered scenarios and their original form" (Taylor, 1991, p. 313). This being so, Harré's neo-Vygotskian developmental sequence may be interpreted (especially the stages of transformation and publication) as processes in which individuals gradually find their own voices as interlocutors, realizing possibilities inherent in conversations experienced, by virtue of the dialogical forms of these conversations and their appropriations.

Taylor's work enables a fuller appreciation of the richness of conversations and their developmental legacy to those who experience them. In particular, it serves to highlight the practical, as well as the conceptual, understandings that dialogical experience makes available.

THERAPEUTIC CONVERSATIONS

As stated in chapter 1, *psychological therapy is a unique form of conversation that attempts to alter the personal theories about themselves, others, and their own life circumstances that clients have acquired through their participation in other (previous and ongoing) intimate, social, and cultural conversations.* By this time, it should be clear that the conception of conversation being proposed includes those sets of practical activities that typically accompany verbal and nonverbal conversational interactions among individuals in particular societies and cultures. The therapeutic conversation is embedded in other past, ongoing, and anticipated conversations in which both clients and therapists reside and through which they both develop and express themselves. As a conversation, psychotherapy and its products (i.e., psychotherapeutic experience and change) are as amenable to explanation through a Vygotskian historical-cultural, developmental analysis as any other conversations and individual/collective change processes and mechanisms. Other than the somewhat unique aspect of therapeutic conversations and products that places them in a corrective or ameliorative relationship to other conversations and their products, there would seem to be little reason to assume that the developmental schema articulated by Vygotsky, and elaborated and extended by Harré and Taylor, cannot be used to explicate the construction of psychotherapeutic change.

Thus, the theory of therapeutic change presented and supported herein assumes a neo-Vygotskian template with respect to the interrelations and interfunctions of therapeutic, social conversation and a client's cognitive, experiential, and personal change — change that ultimately can affect the client's active, practical engagement in extratherapeutic contexts. Therapeutic conversations are the verbal and nonverbal exchanges and activities that occur between therapists and clients during the course of psychotherapy. Embedded in the therapeutic conversation are the intentions, meanings, and theoretical commitments of the interactors.

Clients come to therapy driven by angst derivative from difficulties in coping with current life circumstances or achieving desired goals. Elaboration of clients' concerns and situations occurs through the vehicle of the therapeutic conversation. Through conversation, a therapist and client agree to direct their activities toward certain ends, to divide their labor and responsibility in particular ways, and come to respect and trust each other (cf. Horvath & Greenberg, 1986). Once such conditions are in place, the therapeutic conversation may be viewed as a joint, social construction or narrative of the client's current and past experiences, difficulties, understandings, imaginings, and hopes. A wide variety of discourse such as storytelling, analogy, metaphor, imagery, and argument typically are employed in a shared effort to portray the client's experiential world as fully as possible. Personal meanings, attitudes, values, beliefs, and desires are articulated and explored. Both conversationalists offer interpretations that recognize patterns of perception, understanding, and action that seem relevant to the issues under discussion. In many forms of therapy, particular emphasis is placed on the client's active involvement in the generation and maintenance of such patterns. Depending on the form of therapy undertaken, the conversation may be replete with roleplays, experiential exercises, systematic record keeping, emotionally laden reminiscences, rational analyses, and other social, interpersonal variations. Such activities augment both the conceptual and practical richness of the therapeutic exchange that is made available to clients.

Following the developmental template adopted by Vygotsky (1934/ 1986) and Harré (1984), the primary function of the therapeutic conversation, whatever its form, variations, or characteristics, is its internalization (appropriation) by the client. As the therapeutic conversation unfolds, it becomes available to the client as content and forms for inner speech (verbal thought), and the construction of psychological tools (understandings, strategies, and practices). The outward, interpsychological relations become the inner, intrapsychological, mental functions. With this internalization, "two important processes are interwoven: the transition from external communication to inner dialogue, and the expression of intimate thoughts in linguistic form, thus making them communicative" (Kozulin, 1986, p. xxxviii).

Obviously, young persons and adults in psychotherapy already have internalized countless conversations, or parts thereof, by virtue of their past social experiences. Consequently, internalizations from the therapeutic conversation are set against previously internalized conceptual frameworks, understandings, practices, and strategies for action. What is internalized from the therapeutic conversation may be capable of amending or forcing revision of a client's existing understandings, frameworks, practices, and strategies, and eventually of supporting different forms of extratherapeutic acting. The extent of such change undoubtedly is a function of numerous factors, several of which will be discussed in the next two chapters of this book. For the present purposes, the critical point is that the foundational mechanism of therapeutic change is the Vygotskian-like internalization of therapeutic conversations by the client. Of particular importance are possibilities for altered perception, understanding, and action contained in these internalizations.

EMPIRICAL EVIDENCE

The plausibility of clients' internalization of therapeutic conversations as a significant determinant of therapeutic change is supported in several ways by research conducted by myself and my colleagues, and by other researchers of psychotherapeutic change.

Own Research

Much of the research on therapeutic change with which I have been associated involves the intensive study of actual therapeutic conversations and the gathering of recollections, interpretations, and ratings of clients and therapists immediately following (and sometimes at later intervals) the conclusion of individual therapy sessions. So as to support the central notion of clients' internalization or appropriation of therapeutic conversations as a critical component of my theory of therapeutic change, I want to focus here on specific results obtained in a subset of research of this kind.

In an exploratory, theory-generation study, Karl Stelmaczonek and

I (Martin & Stelmaczonek, 1988, Study 1) attempted to understand better the kinds of events during psychotherapy that clients regarded as especially important. Therapists and clients in eight short-term therapeutic dyads (eight sessions each) were interviewed by a research assistant immediately following the completion of each therapy session and asked to recall "the most important things that happened during this session." Participants' descriptions of these important events were content analyzed by Karl and a research assistant, working independently of each other. Based on these analyses, the participant-identified important events were coded into categories, many of which were borrowed from Mahrer and Nadler's (1986) system of "good moments" in psychotherapy. This system was used because several of its categories so aptly captured the content descriptions of important events articulated by Karl and the research assistant.

Both therapists and clients most frequently recalled as important six categories of therapeutic events, which I subsequently organized into two major task areas (Martin, 1992). Four types of events related to the therapeutic task of *enhancing clients' personal awareness* are: (1) experiencing a good therapeutic relationship, (2) experiencing and exploring feelings, (3) elaborating personal meanings, and (4) attaining personal insight. The remaining two types of events related to the therapeutic task of *revising personal theories*: (1) internalizing therapeutic processes and constructions, and (2) experimenting with, or experiencing, new ways of behaving and being. Thus, I interpreted results from the first study in Martin and Stelmaczonek (1988) to demonstrate a constructive therapeutic process involving the promotion of clients' awareness of current (and presumably dysfunctional) personal theories, and subsequent revision (reconstruction or restructuring) of these personal theories (presumably with more functional consequences). In many ways, this study constituted the beginning of my adoption of the basic template for therapeutic change presented in the first chapter of this book. The fact that clients in this study were able to identify specific events from psychotherapy sessions with considerable detail and accuracy, together with the nature of the events recalled as important, warranted the interpretation that these clients were internalizing specific parts of the therapeutic conversations in which they were involved and were using such internalizations to reconstruct certain aspects of their personal theories and to experiment with new ways of behaving.

The accuracy with which clients were able to describe specific parts of therapeutic conversations in the first Martin and Stelmaczonek (1988) study came as a surprise to me and other members of the research team. It is a well known finding in cognitive psychological research conducted in laboratory and analogue settings that individuals' memories for particular events can be quite inaccurate, even at rather brief intervals following the occurrence of the events recalled (cf. Ashcraft, 1989). Clearly, clients' internalization of therapeutic events during real-life psychotherapy is a more vivid, more memorable process, presumably because the conversational events experienced during psychotherapy are part of significant identity projects (i.e., self-change and self-development projects) for the clients involved. (In the next chapter, I will have much more to say about the accuracy and longevity of clients' memories of therapeutic conversational episodes.)

The ability of clients in the study described above (as well as in subsequent studies by Martin, Paivio, and Labadie, 1990; Cummings, Hallberg, Martin, and Slemon, 1992; and Cummings, Martin, Hallberg, and Slemon, 1992) to identify and recall specific events during psychotherapy (including actual words and gestures exchanged during therapeutic conversations) is quite remarkable. Such results provide initial support for a theory of therapeutic change that emphasizes clients' internalization of therapeutic conversations as a main element in this change process.

A subsequent study conducted by Martin, Paivio, and Labadie (1990) employed a similar methodology to that used by Martin and Stelmaczonek (1988). In this study we explored relative contributions of clients and therapists to the therapeutic events that clients internalized, as evidenced by their accurate postsession recall of specific elements from therapeutic conversations during these events. A more detailed report of this study appears in chapter 3. However, for the current purposes, it is instructive to note that, in this investigation, it was therapists' contributions to the therapeutic conversation, not clients' contributions, that distinguished events that clients recalled as important from matched control events from the same therapy sessions. The strong implication of this finding is that therapists' contributions to therapeutic conversations may be especially influential in determining what clients take from these conversations. The Vygotskian idea of private human development as stimulated by the internalization of public, social, and linguistic forms seems an apt interpretation of such findings.

Such an interpretation is strengthened further by noting a heretofore unpublicized finding from the Martin and Stelmaczonek (1988), Martin, Paivio, and Labadie (1990), and Cummings, Hallberg, Martin, and Slemon (1992) data sets. While clients' recollection of therapeutic events in these studies was, as already stated, highly accurate and specific, there were obvious errors of recollection evident in approximately 5% to 10% (depending on the specific study) of these recollections. Of these inaccuracies, the most common type involved clients' attribution of the source of conversational comments to themselves rather than to the therapists who actually made the comments in question (as substantiated by videotape recordings and verbatim transcriptions of therapy sessions in these studies). The fact that clients would make this kind of mistake provides additional evidence for a process of internalization of public, social therapeutic conversations into the private, mental constructions of individual clients. In particular, it supports Taylor's (1989, 1991) contention that what is incorporated from conversations is the dialogue in all its richness, not a series of detached monological actions. It also is important to note that many practitioners of psychotherapy (cf. Friedlander, in press) consider clients' adoption of therapists' words and manners as a sign that psychotherapy is progressing well. More formal evidence of such "adoption" appears in analyses of transcriptions from time-limited psychotherapy groups, as reported by Friedlander, Thibodeau, Nichols, Tucker, and Snyder (1985).

A good illustration of how clients in psychotherapy internalize therapeutic conversations, and how such internalizations can become functional psychological tools for clients, occurs in a case study I reported in detail several years ago (cf. Martin, 1987). The client in this case study was a 35-year-old woman who was suffering verbal and physical abuse from a man with whom she lived. Immediately following each of eight sessions of therapy, the woman was asked to free associate to her own name, the name of her partner, brief phrases describing her problems, and possible solutions to her problems. All of the client's associative responses were recorded on gummed labels, one response to a label. These labels then were returned to the client so that she could organize them on a sheet of laminated paper, indicating relationships among the words or phrases contained on the labels by placing related labels in greater physical proximity or by using glass-marking pencils to draw connecting lines between labels.

In this case study, the client's responses to the free association and conceptual mapping tasks clearly revealed her internalization of therapeutic conversations over, and subsequent to, the eight therapy sessions. Following the first session of therapy, her conceptual map of her problems consisted of a centrally located, self-referencing label ("me"), connected directly to surrounding labels indicative of negative affect ("hopeless," "trapped," "afraid," "ashamed," "can't do anything right"), and connected indirectly to clusters of labels representing her partner, her children, and her parents, as well as her relationships with them. There was no indication of understanding or insight into her problems or of possible strategies that might be engaged to address her problems. Following eight sessions of psychotherapy, this client produced a conceptual map of her problems that contained clear indications of both enhanced understanding and possible strategies for responding. In this last map, a centrally located, self-referencing label was connected directly to a cluster of labels representing her unwilling participation in a cycle of family violence that represented her partner as a dangerous batterer in need of help. Another cluster of labels, emanating directly from the central self-referencing label, identified strategic options available through a local women's center and through the supportive intervention of her own extended family. Affective labels in this map referred to anger and worry, but also to hope.

Results obtained on the conceptual mapping task employed in this case study, when set against transcriptions and tape recordings of the therapy sessions themselves, indicate a clear relationship between salient conversational themes during the course of therapy and the client's free associative, conceptual mapping responses following the therapy sessions. The therapeutic intervention focused primarily on clarifying and elaborating the client's affective reactions, providing information about relationship violence and men who batter women and the exploration of options that would remove the client from her currently dysfunctional life circumstances. In this case, the conceptual mapping responses of the client were interpreted as evidence of her internalization of these therapeutic conversations into her own personal theory about her problems and possible solutions to them. The eventual ability of this client to extricate herself from the abusive relationship she had endured for so many years, and to make more favorable arrangements for herself and her children, probably was facilitated by this internalization process.

Other Research

Other than the original work reported herein, the researcher of psychotherapy who made the most extensive and explicit use of Vygotsky's ideas concerning the internalization of public conversations was Donald Meichenbaum (1977). In a series of studies conducted in the early 1970s, Meichenbaum demonstrated that it was possible to conduct a form of therapeutic intervention called *self-instruction training* in which clients eventually came to internalize very specific forms of self-regulatory talk.

In self-instruction training, clients initially watch and listen to a therapist who talks aloud while engaging in a particular activity, typically an activity that the client reacts to with fear, misunderstanding, or inappropriate action. After watching and listening to the therapist, the client is coached to engage the task (or some less threatening or less difficult related task) while speaking aloud, using the same words and phrases as used previously by the therapist. Eventually, the client engages the task while speaking covertly, using the now internalized, inner speech as a psychological tool to regulate responses to the targeted task. The numerous experimental studies reported by Meichenbaum and his colleagues (cf. Meichenbaum, 1977; Meichenbaum & Jarmenko, 1983) provide considerable empirical support for the effectiveness of self-instruction training as a specific therapeutic intervention and for the more general notion of the internalization of therapeutic conversations and contents as an important mechanism of therapeutic change.

While the work of Meichenbaum and his colleagues has focused on specific, structured therapeutic interventions that make direct use of Vygotsky's ideas concerning the internalization of public speech, the template for therapeutic change endorsed herein is more general. It considers the client's internalization of therapeutic conversations to be a necessary component in all successful psychotherapy, at least with voluntary clients who are not seriously disturbed in their functioning. In this sense, the conceptualization proposed is more similar to that developed initially by Wexler and Rice (1974) as a theoretical explanation for the conduct and efficacy of experiential, client-centered therapy. This explanation has been elaborated and refined through what has come to be known as the events paradigm for research on therapeutic change (Rice & Greenberg, 1984; Safran, Greenberg, & Rice, 1988).

In an early articulation of this perspective, Zimring (1974) indicated that the goal of client-centered therapy is "an increase in [the client's] experiential organization," and that "the therapist achieves this goal through an interaction involving joint processing of the client's experience. The therapist works both at the same level with and slightly ahead of the client's ability to organize, thus facilitating his processing" (p. 136). In the theoretical language employed in this book, the therapist and client use their conversations during psychotherapy to create a more elaborated, explanatory narrative or theory of the client's current experiences, a theory that is internalized by the client through his or her appropriation of the therapeutic conversation. Once internalized, this theory can act as a basis for more creative, practical responding to relevant extratherapeutic situations. The very nature of the client's experience in the world becomes transformed as the client now uses these newly internalized forms to restructure understandings and beliefs that underlie social perceptions and actions.

Events paradigm research reported by Rice and Saperia (1984) provides a good illustration of empirical work that supports the foregoing perspective on therapeutic change. Rice and Saperia studied client change processes during therapeutic events in which clients described, and attempted to understand, incidents in their lives in which they had found themselves reacting in ways that they found problematic (strange, exaggerated, inappropriate). An example would be a client's continuing remorse and upset about shouting at a waiter in a restaurant who had provided unsatisfactory service, particularly if this specific form of problematic reaction constituted a theme in the client's life experiences.

On the basis of their own clinical experience and observations, Rice and Saperia constructed an idealized "rational performance model" for the therapeutic resolution of such problematic reactions. This model then was elaborated through consideration of additional data. It later was subjected to empirical verification testing, once a battery of measures had been constructed to record features of therapeutic interactions relevant to testing the adequacy of the model. Eventually, a fully articulated model was developed to represent hypothesized change mechanisms undergirding clients' successful resolutions of problematic reactions through therapeutic intervention. This model consisted of a set of tasks to be undertaken so as to enable a therapeutic reexperiencing of the extratherapeutic experiences that the client finds problematic. These tasks involve a detailed examination of both external/situational and internal/experiential features of relevant extratherapeutic experiences and of the subsequent reactions of the client to them. Completion of these therapeutic tasks leads to a reconceptualization of the problematic reactions (culminating in the recognition of patterns involved in reactions of this type) and an exploration of alternative reactions.

Of particular relevance to the internalization of therapeutic conversations, are examples that Rice and Saperia (1984) provide in support of the foregoing pattern of therapeutic work. In an example of a therapeutic conversation concerning the problematic reactions of a busy mother to her children's mealtime behavior, the following exchanges appear:

> C: One of the things that drives me sort of crazy is the kids fooling around when they're eating. . . . And they get up and look out the window and come back and eat, and slowly, like an hour to eat. And I get so furious and so controlling and they have to only eat and no silliness and you know very demanding. And really overreacting to little kids against ordinary manners.
>
> T: Let's make sure that I understand. When the kids are eating and they dawdle and take their time—that just seems to drive you around the bend. And you feel that you're overreacting. (p. 47)

Through a series of such conversational exchanges, the therapist helps the client to elaborate the situation (in this case, mealtimes with her children), her experiences of it, and her reactions to it. The client's experiences in the situation gradually are articulated in a way that constitutes a sort of evocative, experiential unfolding.

> T: Do you have a sense of what that impatience feels like?
>
> C: (long silence) Hmm — It has something to do with feeling the responsibility. And it's at that time I'm feeling that my job, my responsibility, is to be there with the kids, and to prepare lunch. And I separate — I tend to — It's almost like I separate my whole life, or a day or whatever into — little sections. And I can't go on to any section or do anything until one is over. (pause) And I can see that in other things too. I used to draw and paint, and I couldn't start a picture because there were going to be other things that interfered with it, so that meant that I couldn't start it at all.
>
> T: Oh. So by kind of making these little slots for yourself — in a way it — you kind of stop yourself from —
>
> C: I stop myself from doing anything else. And them being silly and taking a long time — they're stopping my life.
>
> T: Oh, I see. If they cooperated, then you could be over and finished with that particular section, and you could feel like you did your job well, and then get on to something else.
>
> C: That's right — (pause). And I think the only times I've really enjoyed having lunch with them is when I've been — when I've been more involved with it and made it part of my life. Almost, as if they were people, rather than seeing it as a job in that slot. (pp. 48–49)

As the conversation continues, more of the client's experiences and reactions are articulated, and greater understanding of these experiences and reactions is fostered through the conversational collaboration of therapist and client. It is through the client's internalization of precisely these conversational elements that the client

> clearly felt better about herself and about the situation. A new option had emerged from her realization that when the children's meals were not construed as belonging to a work section in which she must do nothing but discharge her responsibility as a good mother, she enjoyed their company, and control was no problem. She briefly explores the new option of treating the children as partners rather than viewing them as adversaries, and expresses confidence that they can work it out together. (p. 51)

THEORETICAL COHERENCE

While many psychoanalytic, cognitive, and experiential theories of psychotherapy have incorporated developmental perspectives within their overall theoretical frameworks, relatively few theories of psycho-therapy or psychotherapeutic change have been constructed on the basis of developmental perspectives that have been formulated outside of ex-plicitly psychotherapeutic theorizing. One such previous attempt is found in the work of Allen Ivey (1991). However, unlike the theory of psychotherapeutic change presented here, Ivey's approach is a more dualistic account based on the developmental theories of Piaget. Further, Ivey's work seems more concerned with making recommendations for the actual practice of psychotherapy, as opposed to furnishing a detailed theoretical account of how psychotherapy might work.

There is, nonetheless, a sense in which many analytic, experiential, social, and cognitive approaches to psychotherapeutic practice may be interpreted as assuming some sort of internalization process, perhaps similar to the Vygotskian interpretation offered in this chapter. Unfortu-nately, such assumptions most often are not stated explicitly, nor are they elaborated in any theoretical detail. Rather than adopting a less dualistic account of the internalization of therapeutic conversations as a primary mechanism of therapeutic change, most extant theories of psychotherapy emphasize either the client's internal transformations or the external therapeutic interaction, rather than their interface.

For example, many cognitive theories of therapeutic practice (cf. Dryden & Golden, 1986; Mahoney & Freeman, 1985) consider signifi-cant client change to result from various kinds of schematic restructuring of clients' belief and knowledge systems. However, most of these ap-proaches make no explicit theoretical links between the conceptual con-tent of actual therapeutic conversations and the schematic restructuring assumed. Without any such specification, there remains a mysterious gap between discussions during therapy sessions and clients' extratherapeutic change. Most often, attempts to fill this gap place considerable faith in clients' motivation to change, clients' abilities to transfer conceptual and procedural content through self-control and problem-solving strategies, or clients' enhanced abilities to construe their circumstances and reac-tions in more rational, functional ways. The precise ways in which such motivations and abilities arise from the therapeutic interactions between therapist and client remain mostly unaddressed.

Several experiential approaches to psychotherapeutic change [aside from those of Wexler and Rice (1974), Rice and Greenberg (1984), and others who have conducted fine-grained analyses of relationships among therapeutic discourse and client experiential and cognitive change] also emphasize the clients' internal transformations. In most client-centered, humanistic therapies, the general relationship (construed mostly in af-fective rather than in conceptual terms) between therapist and client is viewed as facilitating natural tendencies of the client to grow and develop in ways that enhance the experiential, extratherapeutic functioning of the client. Here, the therapeutic conversation functions as a safe haven that releases the client's internal potentials for agenic self-development. Once again, exactly how this "release" happens is largely unexplained.

On the other hand, social psychological approaches (cf. Claiborn & Lichtenberg, 1989; Strong, Welsh, Corcoran, & Hoyt, 1992) to theorizing about therapeutic change have tended to emphasize the therapeutic impact of such variables as interpersonal power and intimacy (influence). These variables are clearly resident in interactions between clients and therapists during psychotherapy and are assumed somehow to affect clients' repertoires of interpersonal responses and strategies in extratherapeutic contexts. However, while some relatively recent attempts have been made to integrate social psychological and more cognitive, conceptual perspectives on therapeutic change (e.g., Heppner & Claiborn, 1989), the idea of conversational appropriation or internalization as developed in this chapter is essentially unknown in social psychological analyses of therapeutic change mechanisms. Thus, no plausible explanation as to how changes to clients' repertoires of social responses transfer from therapeutic to extratherapeutic contexts is offered.

Aside from the research reviewed above, there has been little explicit theoretical articulation of the Vygotskian internalization template in mainstream psychotherapy literature. Until recently, detailed empirical, conceptual analyses of therapeutic conversations were almost unknown in research on psychotherapy. Even with increasing popularity, such analyses tend to consist primarily of structural examinations of types and categories of interactive responses (cf. Greenberg & Pinsof, 1986) rather than the sorts of conceptual, developmental analyses described in the empirical work reported herein. When psychotherapy is viewed as a conversation targeted at the amelioration of personal theories (conceptual systems) and practical actions that have been acquired developmentally from clients' experiences in previous and current intimate, social, and cultural conversations, clients' internalization of the therapeutic conversation offers a nondualistic, parsimonious, and sensible account of a primary mechanism of therapeutic change. While relatively unknown in theory and research on psychotherapy, such an analysis has been applied to other areas within what might be termed the psychology of human change, including educational change (e.g., Wertsch, 1991) and self-development (Gergen & Gergen, 1988).

In some ways the neo-Vygotskian perspective adopted here is similar to other, general (i.e., nontherapeutic) developmental theories that emphasize the importance of social, cultural conversations in intellectual and personal development and change. In particular, Jerome Bruner (1986, 1990) considers mind as neither a biological organ nor an information processor, but as a personal representation of interpersonal practices and cultural knowledge. Moreover, Bruner proposes a uniquely human propensity for narrative forms of theorizing as a basis for the development of such personal representations. Thus, for Bruner conversation is a form of narrative construction that becomes internalized in the minds of individual humans. However, unlike Vygotsky (after whom he modeled much of his earlier work), Bruner adopts a quite radical form of cognitive constructivism in which the sufficiently developed mind is capable of transcending conversationally imposed constraints, seemingly without the assistance of facilitative, enabling conditions in the form of alternative, corrective conversational contexts (such as psychotherapy). [Interested readers will find a therapeutic rendering of many of Bruner's ideas in the work of Bonanno (1990).] Where a neo-Vygotskian account permits some individual transcendence of experienced conversational parameters and forms, by virtue of developmental processes of transformation and publication, Bruner's account seems to emphasize a more historically and experientially detached form of transcendence and change, the precise origins of which never are articulated adequately.

It also is important to distinguish the neo-Vygotskian perspective adopted herein from analytic philosophical, ordinary-language accounts of human development, such as that of Wittgenstein (1953). These accounts also emphasize the critical role of practical conversation in human intellectual and personal development. Unlike Bruner's approach, such accounts seem to leave too little room for any sort of socially derivative, psychological transcendence and change. They effectively reduce all thought to functional linguistic forms available in cultural practices. It should be noted that much of Harré's psychological work adopts a strong Wittgensteinian perspective (e.g., Harré, 1992). In using Harré's work in this book, I have borrowed especially from that aspect of his writings that relates to his elaboration of a Vygotskian developmental sequence. I have not adopted his thoroughgoing antimentalism that marks him as a neo-Wittgensteinian.

The neo-Vygotskian perspective on the internalization of conversational forms and content lies nicely between accounts such as those of Bruner and Wittgenstein. It promotes a nonmysterious, socially and historically grounded form of human development that recognizes both the inevitable sameness and the uniqueness of individual experiences within cultures, societies, and interpersonal interactions. It seems true that individuals who experience identical conversational contexts likely will develop in similar ways. However, it seems equally true that no sets of individual conversational histories are likely to be exactly identical. Thus, there is no paradox in holding to a neo-Vygotskian form of social-cultural critical realism, while simultaneously endorsing a constrained form of individual constructivism that arises from transformational and publication processes that occur in the context of "nonduplicated" individual conversational histories.

In the next chapter, an explanation of the mediational means by which therapeutic conversations become internalized into clients' personal theories will be presented. The primary mediational vehicle proposed is clients' episodic memories of specific therapeutic events and content. Extending the Vygotskian template of internalization with perspectives derived from the theoretical and empirical work on episodic memory conducted by Endel Tulving (1983, 1985) and Alan Paivio (1986) makes possible a specific account of therapeutic change mechanisms that enables both "the transition from external communication to inner dialogue, and the expression of intimate thoughts in linguistic form" (Kozulin, 1986, p. xxxviii).

Chapter 3

MEMORIES

As far as we know, members of no other species possess
quite the same ability to experience again now, in a different situation and perhaps in a different form, happenings
from the past, and know that the experience refers to an
event that occurred in another time and in another place.
(E. Tulving, 1983, p. 1)

Memory for past experience is called *episodic* memory. This is the
meaning of memory that is assumed in most uses of ordinary language.
Yet, until the early 1970s, episodic memory received little attention from
psychologists and other social scientists. In this chapter, I use conceptual
and empirical work by Tulving (1983, 1985) and Paivio (1971, 1986) as a
basis for elaborating the Vygotskian notion of internalization, especially
with respect to psychotherapeutic change. Such a strategy enables conceptual connections between much psychotherapeutic theorizing about
the role of memory in human change and contemporary psychological
research in the areas of memory and cognition.

Historically, memory for specific life events has played an important role in psychotherapeutic theory. Psychoanalytic therapy, in particular, was conceptualized by Freud (1900/1955, 1917/1966, 1918/1966)
as a process of uncovering repressed memories, reexperiencing the events
symbolized in these memories, and thus freeing clients from their dysfunctional influence. Whether or not one interprets clients' memories of
their earlier life experiences as veridical, Freudian theory demands a
narrative account of clients' current psychological functioning in terms
of their experiential memories of past events in their lives (cf. Spence,
1984). From this perspective, psychotherapy may be interpreted as requiring the construction of such narratives, the internalization of which

enables the attainment of *insight* that leads to the revision of clients' personal theories of themselves and their difficulties.

As Rorty (1991a) has noted:

> By turning the Platonic parts of the soul into conversational partners for one another, Freud did for the variety of interpretations of each person's past what the Baconian approach to science and philosophy did for the variety of descriptions of the universe as a whole. He let us see alternative narratives and alternative vocabularies as instruments for change, rather than as candidates for a correct depiction of how things are in themselves. (p. 152)

Under this interpretation, the therapeutic process is not so much a matter of "lifting" repressions as primarily a means of providing clients with empowering and humanizing experience (Bonanno, 1990). In what follows, I will argue that it is through the mediation of memories of the therapeutic experience itself that functional accommodations to clients' personal theories are accomplished.

It is critical to note that *two* distinctive types of episodic memory are intertwined in the interpretation of therapeutic change adopted herein. One is the client's in-therapy recollection of past life events and experiences. The other is the client's extratherapeutic recollection of therapeutic conversations and experiences. The former functions to elaborate and extend the client's understanding of focal problems and concerns. The latter is necessary for the internalization of therapeutic conversations and experiences, so that such information might mediate revisions to the client's personal theories and future, extratherapeutic actions. Both of these functions of episodic memory will be elaborated in this chapter.

By employing episodic memory for life experiences and therapeutic conversations as a fundamental mediational mechanism (psychological tool) for therapeutic change, I combine theoretical perspectives from cognitive psychology (Tulving, 1983, 1985), social developmental psychology (Harré, 1984; Vygotsky, 1934/1986), and psychoanalysis (Bucci, 1985; Freud, 1917/1966). To render such a theoretical integration intelligible, I begin this chapter with an account of the theory of episodic memory developed by Endel Tulving (1983, 1985). I then elaborate this account with a discussion of the dual-coding theory of human memory developed by Alan Paivio (1971, 1986). These discussions lead to a theoretical description of episodic memory mediation in therapeutic change and then to a discussion of empirical and conceptual work that supports and tests various aspects of this account.

TULVING'S THEORY OF EPISODIC MEMORY

Tulving (1983) posits the existence of three separate memory systems: (1) *procedural* memory, (2) *semantic* memory, and (3) *episodic* memory. The three systems are related to each other in that procedural memory (the most developmentally basic or foundational form of memory) "contains semantic memory as its single specialized subsystem. . . . Semantic memory, in turn, contains episodic memory as its single specialized subsystem" (Tulving, 1985, p. 387). Each more specialized memory system depends on (is supported by) the more general, more foundational system or systems. However, each of the more specialized memory systems possesses capabilities not possessed by the more general systems. Thus, while semantic memory is a subsystem of procedural memory, it is a subsystem that envelops and encases the foundational procedural system. Similarly, episodic memory envelops and encases the semantic system. It is important to note that episodic memory, the most personalized memory system, develops out of the procedural and semantic systems. This important aspect of Tulving's theory makes it potentially amenable to the general developmental perspective of Vygotsky, one that views the personal and private as developing out of an internalization of more social, public forms of perception and meaning.

Tulving makes it very clear that each successive memory system is characterized by unique capabilities *not* possessed by the more foundational system(s).

> Procedural memory enables organisms to retain learned connections between stimuli and responses, including those involving complex stimulus patterns and response chains, and to respond adaptively to the environment. Semantic memory is characterized by the additional capability of internally representing states of the world that are not perceptually present. It permits the organism to construct mental models of the world . . . models that can be manipulated and operated on covertly, independently of any overt behavior. Episodic memory affords the additional capacity of acquisition and retention of knowledge about *personally experienced events* and their temporal relations in subjective time and the ability to mentally "travel back" in time. (p. 387, italics added)

Mental representations in procedural memory are believed to consist of propositions that link various actions to conditions with which they are associated. The procedural memory system thus provides blueprints for future action without really containing any explicit information about the past (Dretske, 1982). Representations in the semantic memory system contain propositions that describe the world without prescribing any particular actions or taking any particular attitude with respect to these descriptions. The important points to note are that representations in both the procedural and semantic systems are depersonalized and generally similar in content to the socially available information they represent (Dretske, 1982).

In a way that is quite distinct from the other two memory systems, the information contained in episodic memory goes beyond representations of condition-action rules and declarative propositions to include schematic relations of this information to the rememberer's *personal identity*. My recollection of my childhood experience of humiliation on the occasion of my failure to receive a passing certificate from my swimming instructor at a public presentations ceremony (described in chapter 1) is a good example of an episodic memory. My episodic memory system also includes vivid recollections of my feelings and experiences of loneliness at the beginning of my first year "away from home" during my freshman year at university, of success on "making" a varsity athletics team, of extreme nervousness on the occasion of my first interview for an academic position, of happiness and trepidation as I turned to meet my wife at our marriage ceremony, and of a multitude of other personally significant life experiences.

The episodic memory system is unabashedly subjective in much of its content and in the framing of this content within subjective time and space (Tulving, 1983). Two extremely important consequences follow from this recognition of the subjective, experiential nature of episodic memory. These consequences concern the type of knowledge expression and consciousness associated with episodic memory in comparison with procedural and semantic memory.

Only direct, nonreflective expression of knowledge is possible in procedural memory. Relatively rigid condition-action rules generally restrict the expression of procedural knowledge to formats determined at the times these rules were acquired. On the other hand, acquired knowledge in the semantic memory system can be expressed more flexibly in different behavioral forms and under conditions quite removed from those of original learning. However, such flexibility in knowledge expression still is governed by relatively formal rules concerning patterns of association and activation within relevant declarative, propositional networks. Both procedural and declarative memory systems restrict knowledge expression to information that is, for the most part, readily available in the public domain to all members of a particular social-cultural group.

Unlike knowledge expression in these foundational memory systems, the mode of knowledge expression in episodic memory is a form of recollective and/or projective experiencing that is thought to be associated intimately with the *attitude* of an individual knower (cf. Bartlett, 1932; Tulving, 1983, 1985). What this means is that information internalized in episodic memory can be reflected on in a self-conscious manner capable of temporally bridging past, present, and future. As illustrated by my episodic memories of my childhood, university, academic, and marital experiences, episodic memories are memories for past experiences that can be recollected and projected forward in time to inform and motivate current and future courses of action, especially if personal attitudes associated with the recollections motivate such projection. Knowledge in episodic memory schemas is known by the rememberer. It is historic, experiential, autobiographical, and laden with personal meanings and affect. The uniquely human character of the schematic associations in episodic memory provides a framework for the interface of personality, affect, and motivation.

As should be clear by now, the kind of consciousness associated (actually and/or potentially) with episodic memory is highly distinctive from the forms of consciousness associated with the procedural and semantic memory systems. Procedural memory is associated with *anoetic* (nonknowing) consciousness. Anoetic consciousness refers to an organism's capability of sensing and reacting to external and internal stimulus patterns. Semantic memory is associated with *noetic* (knowing) consciousness. Noetic consciousness refers to an organism's knowledge of its world. It makes possible an introspective awareness of both internal and external worlds. Episodic memory is associated with *autonoetic* (self-knowing) consciousness. As implied earlier, this sort of consciousness involves the personal awareness of a knower of

> his or her own identity and existence in subjective time that extends through the present to the future. It provides the familiar phenomenal flavor of recollective experience characterized by "pastness" and subjective veridicality. (Tulving, 1985, p. 388)

The self-knowing consciousness resident in episodic memory has particular relevance to psychotherapy. It would be difficult to imagine a client seeking psychotherapy in the absence of a sense of "self." Increased understanding of oneself and one's experience is almost always a major goal in psychotherapy.

As Tulving (1983) speculates, an individual's personal identity seems grounded in episodic memories of past experiences. To support this conjecture, Tulving (1983) describes the actual case of a 21-year-old man who reported to a hospital because "he did not know who he was. He did not know his name or address, and had great difficulty remembering anything from his past" (p. 96). Since the young man's amnesia cleared up after a few days in the hospital, it was possible for Tulving and his colleagues to test this man's semantic and episodic memories both during and after his bout with amnesia. The test of semantic memory involved showing him photographs of famous people and asking him to identify them. The patient did equally well on this test during and after the amnesia. The test of episodic memory required the young man to provide personal experiences in response to single cue words. During the amnesia, only 14% of the patient's responses were drawn from his personal experiences prior to the onset of his amnesia (most of these were from a single "island" of memory from his past that somehow was unaffected by the amnesia). However, following the lifting of his amnesia, 92% of the patient's recollections were of events in his life prior to the onset of his amnesia.

What is striking about the foregoing case experiment conducted by Tulving and his colleagues is the association it supports between one's sense of self and the possession of episodic memories of one's past. It is difficult not to be reminded of the popular story line in much current science fiction, in which individuals lose their sense of self as a consequence of manipulations to their experiential memories. Nonetheless, it is not clear whether Tulving himself equates the possession of episodic memories with a sense of self. Within the neo-Vygotskian template adopted in this book, it is, however, tempting to conclude that it is through the accumulation of episodic memories (of conversations experienced over the course of a lifetime) that an individual develops (internalizes) knowledge of "self." In the succeeding chapter, I will argue that such knowledge, organized in personal theories, likely provides a basis for much of one's current and future experiences and actions.

In his writings, Tulving (1983, 1985) presents numerous conceptual and empirically based arguments attesting to the existence of episodic memory as separate and distinct from procedural and semantic memory systems, including a comprehensive rendering of related arguments by others (e.g., Wood, Ebert, & Kinsbourne, 1982). Interested readers are directed to these sources for details of Tulving's defense of his theory. However, a brief description of some additional empirical work by Tulving and his associates should convey the overall nature of the empirical support he offers for a separation of episodic from semantic memory.

Such evidence is important given that many cognitive psychologists and scientists tend to equate semantic and episodic memory, and fail to recognize important ways in which the latter "goes beyond" the former (cf. Tulving, 1983). For example, Anderson (1983) considers three forms of mental representation (temporal string, spatial image, and abstract proposition), but never once alludes to the possible role of any of these representational units with respect to remembering the kind of episodic, experiential information described and illustrated above. Alternatively, Paivio (1986), in discussing the latest version of his dual-coding theory of mental representations (i.e., images and verbal representations), is explicit in discussing the ways in which his imaginal system might be especially suited to the retention of experiential, affectively laden episodic information. A reasonable hypothesis concerning those cognitive scientists who embrace episodic memory as a distinctive kind versus those who do not is that the latter are much more strongly attached to a form of theorizing that takes contemporary computers as a strong source analogy for human cognitive functioning. The more holistic, affective, conative, experiential, and autonoetic features of episodic memory as articulated by Tulving and Paivio are unique to human functioning and have not been simulated in computer environments.

At any rate, with respect to further empirical support for Tulving's theory, Tulving, Schacter, and Stark (1982) compared recognition memory and fragment completion (a form of prompted recall) responses of subjects who one week previously had "learned" lists of words. Results indicated stochastic independence between scores on the recognition task (a task requiring recall of a specific learning episode) and scores on the fragment completion task (a task requiring much less, if any, recall of a specific learning episode). Such separation in task scores may be interpreted to imply a similar separation in the memory systems that are theorized to undergird responses to the different tasks. Tulving (1985) reports three other experiments yielding similar results. He also offers additional evidence for the separation of episodic and semantic memory systems that arises from numerous clinical studies (in addition to the case discussed previously) conducted with brain-damaged individuals who can acquire semantic knowledge with seemingly no ability to recall the learning episodes during which such knowledge was imparted (e.g., Glisky, Schacter, & Tulving, 1984).

For the current purposes, the importance of Tulving's conception of episodic memory lies in its ability to capture and hold subjective experiences of individuals that are replete with accompanying affect and personal meaning and are related to significant identity projects. As mentioned previously, I want to argue that such memories mediate between individuals' experiences of life and therapeutic conversations, and their incorporation of these experiences into personal theories about themselves, others, and their own circumstances. Thus, episodic memory may be seen as an essential vehicle for the Vygotskian internalization of therapeutic conversations. Such internalization may assist clients to develop and elaborate personal theories that are more functional with respect to the concerns and problems that beset them.

A major difficulty that attends any attempt to apply Tulving's work on episodic memory to an enhanced understanding of therapeutic change is that our personal theories often are very informal. They are based on internalizations of previously experienced life events and conversational forms, many of which never have been fully expressed in verbal form or manifest explicitly in verbal thought (see "The Vygotskian Alternative" in chapter 2). Consequently, clients' episodic recollections of many earlier life experiences may influence directly their current ways of attempting to resolve or cope with their difficulties, and yet prove to be extremely difficult to express in verbal form so that they may become elaborated and better understood in therapeutic conversations. Given that in-therapy recollection and articulation of earlier life events and experiences that may exist only in images, sensations, and practical actions frequently are necessary for the therapeutic elaboration and revision of clients' stories and theories, it is necessary to supplement Tulving's account of episodic memory with an explicit account of how nonverbal experiences and their recollection might become part of therapeutic conversations that rely predominantly on verbal means of communication. Exactly such a supplementary account is provided in Alan Paivio's (1971, 1986) dual-coding theory of mental representations.

PAIVIO'S DUAL-CODING THEORY

Dual-coding theory enables an explication of both unconscious/ tacit and conscious/explicit levels of human cognition and memory. The precise manner in which the theory accomplishes this multilevel explication will be the primary focus in the following discussion.

Dual-coding theory places much emphasis on a basic qualitative distinction in types of mental representations and the processes that operate on them (see Paivio, 1986, p. 70). In dual-coding theory, nonverbal (sensorimotor, perceptual, imaginal) and verbal (symbolic, linguistic) inputs are stored in functionally independent, but interconnected memory systems. The nonverbal system incorporates input from any sensory channel (auditory, kinesthetic, olfactory, visceral, visual, savory, tactile), although visual information may predominate in sighted individuals. Thus, in dual-coding theory, the concept of *imagery* connotes nonverbal and includes much more than visual information per se.

Three different kinds of mental processing are assumed in dual-coding theory. *Representational* processing is the relatively direct activation of verbal representations by linguistic stimuli and of nonverbal representations by nonlinguistic stimuli. *Associative* processing refers to the activation of representations within either system by other same-system representations. Both representational and associative processing preserve the functional independence of the verbal and nonverbal representational systems. However, a third type of processing, *referential,* involves the activation of the nonverbal system by verbal stimuli or of the verbal system by nonverbal stimuli. Imaging to words illustrates the former case. Naming objects or pictures illustrates the latter case.

It is important to note the "indirectness" of referential processing. For example, in object naming, objects must first activate imaginal representations in the nonverbal system before system crossover activation of related verbal representations in the verbal system can occur and naming can be accomplished. In imaging to words, the direction of the referential crossover is reversed, with the words activating verbal representations before related imaginal representations can be activated and experienced as images.

Of particular relevance for current purposes are four specialized characteristics of Paivio's (1986) dual memory systems and processing triune. These concern relationships between affect and the nonverbal system, affect and consciousness, agency and cognitive construction, and the functional specializations of the verbal and nonverbal systems.

Affect and the Nonverbal System

"Affective and emotional reactions, being nonverbal by definition must be identified theoretically with the nonverbal representational system and, therefore, they would be expected to accompany such nonverbal cognitive reactions as imagery" (Paivio, 1986, p. 78). Psychotherapy inevitably involves the exploration of affective concerns and emotional reactions as clients struggle with angst generated from their inabilities to resolve or cope successfully with current life circumstances in ways that allow them to construct and attain personally meaningful, desired goals. Because the socially constructed conversation between therapist and client during psychotherapy is largely verbal, the only way these social exchanges can influence the client's nonverbal affective and emotional reactions is through some form of referential processing. The precise manner in which social therapeutic conversations can promote client referential processing thus becomes an important area for theorizing about psychotherapeutic change.

Affect and Consciousness

With respect to the relationship between cognition and affect, dual-coding theory holds that affective responses may follow prior cognitive (not necessarily verbal) identification of a stimulus. However, "the theory also readily handles the reverse causal relationship in which an emotional state, however aroused, increases the probability that relevant images or verbal reactions also will be activated" (Paivio, 1986, p. 80). Note that in this latter case, it is entirely conceivable that representational and associative processing could be confined entirely to the nonverbal system, with no referential bridging to the verbal system and therefore no verbal, conscious access to the emotional experience. This theoretical observation implies that a client's emotional reactions may be associated lawfully with specific nonverbal representations that might be activated by nonverbal processing, completely outside of the client's verbal, conscious awareness.

It also should be noted that self-reflective consciousness *may* occur in the nonverbal system. Possible examples might include processes of mental rotation, image scannings, and symbolic comparisons studied in experimental settings by Shepard (1984), Kosslyn (1980), and others. However, all such processes have been studied under conditions of verbal instructions delivered to experimental subjects that demand the performance of nonverbal mental tasks. Consequently, such tasks (at least as studied experimentally) constitute examples of referential processing between verbal and nonverbal systems, in addition to associative processing within the nonverbal system alone. Further, it is extremely difficult to imagine self-reflective, conscious processing of emotional material in the nonverbal system in the absence of some sort of verbal mediation through the labeling or verbal description of emotional states. Consequently, it seems reasonable to conclude that conscious examination of nonverbal, emotional material requires some sort of referential connection to the verbal system, at least in the great majority of cases.

Agency and Cognitive Construction

Both verbal and nonverbal information is organized or reorganized actively (constructively) by individuals. This proposition implies that clients in psychotherapy are intentional agents capable, under certain supportive conditions, of reorganizing and revising their memories and experiential knowledge/theoretical structures. Presumably, certain forms of social interaction during psychotherapy might be identified as supportive or influential with respect to such reconstructive activity. However, in keeping with the relatively nondualistic position taken in the current rendering of therapeutic change, it is important to emphasize that it is the social conversation (and accompanying activities) of psychotherapy that enables a client's cognitive constructions, as manifest in personal theories and actions based on these theories. Without such social induction, clients would be limited in their constructive possibilities to previously internalized understandings and perspectives.

System Specialization

Verbal and nonverbal organizations and processes differ in at least one important additional way. The "verbal system is specialized for sequential processing, whereas the nonverbal system is specialized for synchronous or parallel processing of multiple representational units. The verbal system generates sequential structures and the nonverbal system generates synchronous (including spatial) structures, with the paradigm cases being their manifestation in speech and compound visual images, respectively" (Paivio, 1986, p. 71). Psychotherapeutic implications of these observations are somewhat speculative. However, since clients' emotional reactions are likely to be largely nonverbal, and therefore processed synchronously, such reactions may be especially difficult to describe verbally. Consequently, types of social, therapeutic interactions between therapists and clients capable of encouraging such expression, with as little loss of personal meaning as possible, may be particularly important to discover and identify.

In general, Paivio's dual-coding theory indicates that clients' episodic memories of both extratherapeutic and therapeutic experiences may be held in verbal and nonverbal forms. Psychotherapy is predominantly a verbal conversation that attempts to address clients' affective, experiential concerns. Paivio's articulation of possible relationships between verbal and nonverbal representations is directly relevant to my consideration of episodic memory as a primary mechanism of internalization, mediating between therapeutic conversations and clients' personal theories and associated actions.

Together, Tulving's theory of episodic memory and Paivio's dual-coding theory of mental representations enable a more precise, feasible account of the Vygotskian idea of internalization than has previously been offered. Furthermore, both theories seem to possess characteristics that make them especially relevant to understanding processes and mechanisms of psychotherapeutic change that inevitably seem to involve self-exploration and understanding of verbal and nonverbal, past and current experiences. While retaining much of the dualism of Piaget and Freud, these accounts nonetheless can be used as a basis for demystifying the manner in which internalization of the social/public into the personal/private might occur. Further, even if Tulving's attempt to cast episodic memory as a separate, distinct memory system ultimately cannot be sustained (and perhaps must give way to a more holistic view of a single memory with episodic aspects), his discussion of episodic elements and functions in human memory likely will stand as a major contribution to any psychology that attempts to understand the bridge between public and private experience.

EPISODIC MEMORIES OF THERAPEUTIC AND EXTRATHERAPEUTIC CONVERSATIONS

The theory of therapeutic change that I now wish to develop further emphasizes (1) clients' internalization of therapeutic conversations, (2) the revision to clients' personal theories (of self and problems/concerns) that accompanies and follows upon this internalization, and (3) the important mediating role played by clients' episodic, experiential memories in facilitating processes of both internalization and revision. Therapeutic conversations serve to elaborate more fully, and with greater meaning, the client's existing theories and knowledge with respect to currently experienced problems and concerns. This elaboration takes place in the public, social arena of psychotherapy. To enable such elaboration, the therapeutic conversation must somehow permit the client to access more fully episodic memories of previous, extratherapeutic experiences relevant to current problems and concerns, so that these can become a more explicit part of the therapeutic social construction (or telling) of the clients' theories (stories). Once this social, public therapeutic elaboration has occurred, together with whatever enhanced understandings might accompany it, the client can internalize it (or significant parts of it) into his or her private, cognitive structures (forms). Revisions to clients' relevant personal theories and the actions they support inevitably occur as existing personal theories are forced to accommodate to the internalization of these therapeutically induced elaborations. Thus, clients' episodic memories serve as critical mediators for the processes of both (1) *social, public theory elaboration* and (2) *cognitive, private theory revision*.

Memory-Mediation of Theory Elaboration

The therapeutic task of social, public theory elaboration is marked by the co-construction of a therapeutic conversation between therapist and client that attempts to describe the client's concerns and related personal theories and knowledge (including attitudes, beliefs, values, and desires). Discourse such as storytelling, interpretation, illustration, analogy, metaphor, imagery, and argument typically are employed in a joint effort to portray the client's experiential world as fully as possible. Personal meanings, attitudes, values, beliefs, desires, and habitual actions are explored and articulated, even though they heretofore may have been "held in mind" tacitly, nonverbally, or subconsciously. As Paivio (1986) has demonstrated, vivid, concrete, imagery-laden language (typical of the sort of highly figurative, experiential language employed in psychotherapy) can enable cross-referential mental processing and therefore verbalization and conscious awareness of material previously stored only in nonverbal, imaginal representations. Interpretations of the client's elaborated, experiential narrative are sought that recognize patterns of perception, understanding, and action that point to the client's personal theories about self and circumstances that seem relevant to focal concerns and issues under discussion.

The retrieval and discussion of clients' episodic memories of extratherapeutic experiences invariably play a critical mediational role in the public, therapeutic elaboration of clients' personal stories. Some approaches to psychotherapy emphasize the recollection and examination of episodic memories from childhood and adolescence (e.g., psychoanalysis), while others emphasize the recollection and examination of relatively current experiences and situations (e.g., behavioral therapies). Whatever the approach taken, the in-therapy accessing and discussion of such memories provides necessary content for therapeutic conversations about the extratherapeutic circumstances and experiences with which clients are concerned.

But if therapeutic conversations are to succeed in elaborating clients' personal theories with respect to their problems and concerns, they must do more than enable the access and discussion of episodic memories readily available to the clients' conscious, verbal faculties. Somehow therapeutic conversations must succeed in elaborating clients' theories in ways previously unavailable to clients, yet in ways that are veridical with clients' own experiences. Since much content in episodic memory is imaginal (scenes, sensations, feelings, perceptions), the retrieval and expression of such content in the verbal, therapeutic conversation provide important opportunities for precisely this type of elaboration. How is this type of experiencing and elaboration possible?

Paivio's (1986) dual-coding notion of referential processing (in particular, imaging to words) is potentially of considerable importance to the elaboration of clients' personal theories in therapeutic conversations.

Recall that in the case of imaging to words, the words must first activate relevant mental representations in the verbal system (representational processing) before intersystem referential links can permit the activation of related imaginal representations in the nonverbal system (referential processing). Paivio also makes it abundantly clear that, based on his and his colleagues' extensive laboratory research, certain types of words are more likely to promote referential processing than others. In particular, experimentation driven by dual-coding theory has found that concrete words tend to promote referential processing activity more than do abstract words. Since psychotherapeutic interactions consist primarily of verbal exchanges, the use of concrete words with reference to specific, extratherapeutic experiences may be more effective than the use of more abstract, conceptual words in promoting more complete referential processing of perceptual, nonverbal memories of these experiences.

To appreciate further the possible therapeutic importance and relevance of the idea that certain forms of language may promote clients' referential activity (and thus enable the episodic recollection of relevant, past extratherapeutic experiences), recall that many theories of psychotherapy hold that much material of therapeutic importance is subconscious or tacit in clients' minds. Both emotional and cognitive factors may prevent accessibility to such memories and the personal knowledge and beliefs associated with them. Emotional factors, particularly those linked to traumatic experiences, may block retrieval of episodic memories (both verbal and nonverbal representations) of past experiences. Such "repression" is, of course, most often, although not solely, associated with psychoanalytic theories of psychotherapy.

Cognitive factors (such as infrequent use, nonelaborative encoding, interference by more recent input, lack of personal knowledge, or inflexible belief systems) also may be implicated in difficulties in retrieving relevant episodic memories as part of the process of public, social elaboration of clients' theories. For example, some cognitive approaches to psychotherapy maintain that tacit, often dogmatically held beliefs frequently are involved in clients' experiences of emotional upset (e.g., Ellis, 1962). Such beliefs are extremely difficult to access consciously. As another example, many forms of experiential (e.g., person-centered and gestalt) therapy assume that both repressed and tacit memories, especially as organized in inaccessible self-theories held by clients, are implicated in clients' rigid, dysfunctional responding (cf. Wexler & Rice, 1974).

Therapeutic encouragement of clients' referential activity may be important in helping clients retrieve unconsciously held (tacit, repressed, or imaginal) episodic memories as part of the prescribed therapeutic work of "personal theory elaboration" in many forms of psychotherapeutic practice. Bucci (1985, pp. 593–597) has explained how the promotion of clients' referential activity in psychoanalytic therapy might enable the therapeutic discussion of previously repressed material. Since episodic schemata in the nonverbal system are more closely linked to affect, such schemata are more vulnerable to repression. The defense system operates to block attention to perceptual representations associated with danger (e.g., "painful" remembered scenes) before these have been acknowledged or labeled explicitly and verbally. However, these repressed, nonverbal memories continue to affect cognition, emotion, and behavior after attention has been withdrawn.

On the other hand, the psychoanalytic interaction between client and therapist takes place in words. Certain therapeutic interventions essential for reality testing operate only in the verbal mode. Thus, perceptual representations must be linked to language in order for structural change in the nonverbal schemata to take place. Verbal references to concrete and perceptual subject matter, by the therapist as well as the client, are particularly well suited to facilitate linkage to the nonverbal schemata, and result in eventual retrieval of repressed memories and material. The treatment goal is to reach representational schemata, stored in episodic memory, that may be nonveridical, nonadaptive, and a source of distress. The psychoanalytic process involves activation of these schemata by free association, interpretation, and other means, and translation of the perceptual episodic memories into external speech. Once expressed in the social, public discourse of psychotherapy, such memories can mediate the elaboration of clients' personal theories of events, themselves, and others, perhaps resulting in cathartic reexperiencing and insight.

At this point, it seems appropriate to draw a distinction between therapeutically productive elaborations of clients' experiential memories of their pasts and the strict veridicality of such memories. While they may underlie personal theories that are especially relevant to client concerns, personal experiential memories may not necessarily be highly accurate recollections of past events as perceived/recalled by others or as set against more "objective" records of these events (e.g., photographs, videotapes, verbatim transcriptions, and so forth). As Loftus (1993) recently has argued, "we do not yet have the tools for reliably distinguishing the signal of true repressed memories from the noise of false ones," and until we do, "psychotherapists, counselors, social service agencies, and law enforcement personnel would be wise to be careful how they probe for horrors on the other side of some presumed amnesic barrier" (p. 534). For particular purposes, such as the use of psychotherapeutic evidence in legal proceedings, Loftus's caution cannot be overstated.

However, for a majority of therapeutic purposes in which well-intended, competent therapists and their clients are attempting to explore memorial and other bases of clients' current understandings, beliefs, and actions so that these can be revised in the service of more functional, adaptive client experience, it probably is not critical to determine precisely the degree of absolute objectivity evident in clients' recollection of their experiential pasts.

Referential activity that enables the articulation of heretofore non-verbal memories of past and extratherapeutic life experiences is not limited to psychoanalytic therapeutic interventions. Similar processes of memory-mediated personal theory elaboration may be at work in both experiential and cognitive psychotherapies. For example, in rational-emotive psychotherapy, concrete descriptions of upsetting emotional experiences can help clients to access specific episodic memories associated with influential, yet tacit beliefs that undergird these dysfunctional emotional reactions. Similarly, Rice and Saperia (1984; see chapter 2) have shown how the use of concrete, intensive analyses of clients' problematic reactions to relatively recent events in their lives can be used in experiential psychotherapy to enhance clients' understanding and resolution of problematic elements in their reactions.

It is important to note that while the changes targeted in such conceptualizations of psychotherapeutic process are internal and private, the therapeutic work that promotes these changes always is social and public. It is the nature of the co-constructed social discourse between therapist and client that either promotes or discourages relevant, episodically mediated elaborations to the client's personal theories. These elaborations occur first in the social, public discourse of psychotherapy before being internalized back into the client's personal, private theories. Clearly, therapists' use of concrete, imagery-rich, specific language may be particularly important in this regard. The discovery of optimally effective therapeutic strategies for influencing desired client referential processing, and verbal recall of heretofore entirely imaginal episodic memories, would seem to be a sensible goal for future social psychological research on psychotherapy.

To date, social psychological research on interpersonal influence in psychotherapy has focused primarily on analyses of social power and intimacy, and the management of congruency and incongruency across the contributions of therapists and clients to the therapeutic interaction (see Yesenosky & Dowd, 1990, for a review of such work). However, the possibility that specific linguistic characteristics of therapeutic discourse might be associated with client change processes has been articulated by a few social psychologists. For example, Watzlawick (1978) referred to metaphor (with its characteristic use of imagery-laden, concrete words) as playing a major part in the "language of change." Such sentiments reflect Frank's (1972) earlier emphasis on persuasive processes in psychotherapy marked by "symbolic communications." Recent research that examines the interpersonal influence that therapists exert on clients' cognitive and memory processes and organizations through the intentional use of specific linguistic constructions such as imagery and metaphor will be reported later in this chapter. But before turning to such research, a more extended conceptualization of how a second form of episodic memory mediation (this time highlighting clients' episodic memories of therapeutic events as opposed to their episodic memories of previous, extratherapeutic experiences) might function to facilitate revisions to clients' private, cognitive theories is necessary to complete a theoretical account of episodic memory as a critical internalization mechanism for both therapeutic and extratherapeutic conversations.

Memory Mediation of Theory Revision

Clients in psychotherapy gradually are helped to retrieve and articulate previously repressed or tacit information from personal episodic memories and to use this information to elaborate their personal theories in public, therapeutic discussions. This "new" information from past, extratherapeutic events and experiences becomes part of the content discussed during the interpersonal, social co-construction of clients' problems, including ways of conceptualizing and acting in relation to these problems.

Individuals are active organizers and construers of social information. Consequently, therapeutic conversations between therapists and clients that refer to elements of previously subconscious material inevitably become encoded and further reconstructed in the minds of clients (and, of course, in the minds of therapists as well). Such intrapersonal "internalization" of the therapeutic conversation constitutes a second form of episodic mediation that leads to the revision of clients' private, personal theories and likely involves mental activation and representation in both verbal and nonverbal memory systems. The central assumption is that certain kinds of therapeutic exchanges and experiences, in interaction with the personal theories of individual clients, have characteristics that make them highly memorable. Such therapeutic elements are encoded and remembered in relation to at least some "core" elements in clients' privately held personal theories. Thus, personal theories of clients that were articulated and elaborated in the public discourse of psychotherapy (with the assistance of episodic recall of previously experienced life episodes) now become part of clients' episodic memories of psychotherapy. These memories of psychotherapy inevitably force some degree of accommodation on clients' relevant personal theories, resulting in revisions to these theories.

The process of social psychological construction in therapy is one in which therapists initially assist clients to change by co-constructing (with clients) social conversations that are meaningful to clients, given their current personal theories. Over time, therapists gradually and incrementally introduce into the social, therapeutic discourse discordant elements (including those from clients' previously unarticulated episodic memories of past, extratherapeutic experiences) that elaborate clients' theories in the public, social arena of psychotherapy. In addition to the therapeutic elaboration of conceptual components of clients' theories, the more practical, "embodied" understandings of clients also can be probed and discussed during psychotherapy. For example, explicit discussion of a client's interpersonal manner and nonverbal presentation may be especially relevant in many instances of psychotherapeutic intervention. Elaboration and revision of such nonverbal, embodied understandings may be facilitated by the therapist's own conversational manner, as well as by more verbal aspects of the psychotherapeutic dialogue. Eventually, clients' memories of psychotherapeutic conversations containing such elaborations, perhaps in concert with contemporary life experiences outside of therapy, enable clients to revise their personal theories of themselves, their circumstances, and their problems.

A number of factors might enhance the memorability for individual clients of various aspects of the therapeutic conversation. Therapeutic dialogue rich in concreteness, vividness, specific illustration, and metaphor (Paivio, 1986; Rummelhart & Norman, 1981) might assist clients' recollections of therapeutic conversations. In addition to such characteristics of therapeutic conversations themselves, two factors that concern the interface between therapeutic conversations and the personal theories of individual clients are likely to be of considerable importance. Research conducted by Pezdek, Whetstone, Reynolds, Askari, and Dougherty (1989) and theoretical work by Mandler (1984) and Loftus and Mackworth (1978) point to a combination of perceived *relevance* and *inconsistency* as critical determinants of episodic, autobiographical memories of everyday experiences. With respect to the account of memory-mediated theory revision being expounded here, it may be that clients both must (1) perceive the potential relevance (importance) of the therapeutic conversation for them and their problems, but also (2) recognize that the manner and content of the therapeutic conversation is somehow inconsistent (discordant) with their current personal theories of themselves and their circumstances. In other words, therapeutic conversations may be most memorable to clients when they are perceived as potentially relevant (helpful, interesting, and so forth), yet somehow different from clients' existing construals of their concerns. Considerable artistry and skill may be required by therapists to monitor clients' current and evolving understandings so that the therapists' own contributions to the therapeutic conversation gradually and incrementally extend, but do not exceed, the capacities for understanding resident in their clients' currently active personal theories.

Over time, clients' memories of therapeutic conversations can act as catalysts to more extensive revision and restructuring of clients' personal theories that might support altered, more adaptive patterns of behavior in relevant extratherapeutic contexts. It is assumed that clients' episodic memories of therapeutic conversations will be held in mind with sufficient salience that a variety of cues encountered in clients' everyday lives can activate them and that such activation gradually will strengthen adaptive revisions to clients' personal theories. It also is assumed that once activated, memories of therapeutic experiences, together with the revised personal theories they foster, can be used by clients as bases for revised patterns of emotional, cognitive, and overt responding in previously problematic life contexts. Dual coding of, and referential access to, memories and theoretical extensions acquired during therapy (possibly as a result of a therapist's use of concrete, imagery-rich, specific language, and interactional factors such as relevance and inconsistency) should increase the likelihood that such personal information will be activated by a wider range of everyday cues than might be the case without such double (experiential/imaginal and verbal/symbolic) representation.

Furthermore, sequential plans of action in verbal memory, and synchronous images of possible consequences of action plans in nonverbal memory (both acquired through memory-mediated internalization of the therapeutic conversation), might equip clients with greater levels of motivation and confidence with respect to extratherapeutic attempts at personal change. One way in which such motivational effects might occur is implied in the work of Markus and Nurius (1986) on "possible selves." These social psychologists argue convincingly that humans have capacities for imagining future scenarios in which they act differently from how they currently do. Such imaginal "projections" can be sources of tremendous motivation and conceptual guidance for efforts at personal change. Therapeutic interventions based on dual-coding theory might be constructed that could influence clients' internal construction and maintenance of such imaginal, future scenarios.

Once again, episodic memory mediation in the model of therapeutic change being presented is a twofold process. First, clients' theories of their problems, their circumstances, and themselves are elaborated in the public conversations that constitute psychotherapy. This elaboration is, in part, fueled by clients' therapy-assisted recall of memories of relevant extratherapeutic experiences from their past and current life experiences. Therapeutic conversations that contain elaborated theories of clients, their problems, and their circumstances then are retained in clients' memories, which (in combination with current and future life experiences) might succeed in mediating similar elaborations to clients' privately held, personal theories. Exactly how such theoretical revision operates, and how it might function to enable altered ways of client experience and action in current and future extratherapeutic contexts, is discussed in the following chapter.

EMPIRICAL EVIDENCE

Empirical tests of the various determinants and mediational functions of clients' episodic memories posited herein have been attempted in a series of studies conducted by myself and my colleagues over the past several years. Less directly related empirical data are available from a small number of studies conducted by others.

Own Research

In chapter 2, results of the first study reported by Martin and Stelmaczonek (1988) were discussed. In this study, the types of therapeutic events recalled by clients immediately following psychotherapy sessions were classified as indicative of *enhanced personal awareness* and *revision of personal theories*. Given that the former classification included events such as experiencing and exploring feelings, and elaborating personal meanings, it is generally consistent with the task of public, social theory elaboration as developed in this chapter. In general, then, the types of episodic memories reported by clients in the first Martin and Stelmaczonek study can be interpreted as supporting the idea that psychotherapy is a memory-mediated process of social, public elaboration and of cognitive, private revision of clients' personal theories that relate to their concerns and goals.

A second study reported by Martin and Stelmaczonek (1988) probed possible conversational determinants of clients' episodic recall of therapeutic events. The specific hypothesis tested was that discourse during events recalled as important by clients would differ from discourse during "control" events drawn from the same therapy sessions in ways consistent with Paivio's (1986) and Tulving's (1983, 1985; Craik & Tulving, 1975) theory and research on "determinants of memorability." Control events were distinctive events, temporally proximate to (but not overlapping with) the client-recalled important events, and matched to the recalled events in terms of length (number of talking turns) and time of interaction. To test the hypothesis, discourse during recalled and control events from three dyads (seven or eight sessions each) was transcribed and coded (by independent raters, blind to event type) on separate six-point rating scales for "depth of meaning," "elaboration of meaning through use of figurative language," "personalizing," "clarity," and "conclusion orientation."

Results of inferential statistical comparisons revealed that client-recalled important therapeutic events were reliably characterized by significantly more "depth of meaning," "elaboration of meaning through use of figurative language," and "conclusion orientation." Thus, the events that clients recalled as important were ones in which therapists and clients attended to the meanings explicit (or implicit) in clients' experiential theories, elaborated these meanings (personal theories) through the use of figurative language (illustrations, images, metaphors, and so forth), and attempted to draw conclusions (i.e., entertained hypotheses and explanations, and formed insights and understandings) concerning clients' experiences.

An additional exploratory component of the second study by Martin and Stelmaczonek (1988) provided information concerning clients' ability to recall, at a 6-month follow-up, events they had recalled as important immediately following the therapy sessions studied. To our knowledge, no one previously had attempted to provide data relevant to this question. The procedure employed was to cue clients' recall (after a 6-month period) by having them view a brief one-minute segment from the start of videotapes of each of the therapy sessions in which they previously had participated. Clients recalled accurately at the 6-month follow-up the exact same events they previously had recalled as important in 73% of the cases tested (40% from the exact therapy sessions cued, 33% from therapy sessions other than those cued). These results stand in startling contrast to results of studies of episodic memories in laboratory and analogue experiments where subjects are asked to recall events of little personal significance to them. In these studies, subjects generally succeed in recalling few such insignificant events, and then with generally poor accuracy (cf. Ashcraft, 1989). Clearly, clients' episodic memories for therapeutic conversations concerning their understanding of their current difficulties and concerns are much more enduring and accurate than individuals' episodic memories for less personally relevant, less meaningful material. Thus, the possibility that clients' episodic memories of psychotherapy might be retained to force accommodation on their personal theories as employed in everyday, extratherapeutic contexts is strengthened by these findings.

We interpreted results from the Martin and Stelmaczonek (1988) studies to lend support to an emerging theory that psychotherapy worked by somehow embedding in the minds of clients relatively lasting episodic memories from therapeutic conversations and interactions that could be used as a basis for the revision of clients' personal knowledge and theories, and eventually to support altered "real-life" experiencing and actions. Further, if results from the hypothesis-testing portion of the second study could be confirmed, it might eventually be possible to identify general characteristics of therapeutic conversations that therapists might be able to manipulate in order to enhance clients' long-term episodic memories of psychotherapy.

Our next study (Martin, Paivio, & Labadie, 1990) was devoted to a verification test of the results obtained from the hypothesis-testing portion of the second Martin and Stelmaczonek (1988) study. In this research, we studied six short-term therapy dyads (8 to 14 sessions each) in which experienced psychotherapists employed either cognitive or experiential forms of psychotherapy. As in Martin and Stelmaczonek (1988), clients recalled important therapeutic events immediately after therapy sessions were completed. Discourse from these events was compared with discourse from same-session control events on the potentially memory-enhancing variables examined in the previous study. Once again, the control events were temporally proximate to the client-recalled important events, but were thematically and strategically distinctive from the client-recalled important events. Control events were matched to the recalled events in terms of elapsed time and number of participants' talking turns.

The psychometric properties of the six-point scales used to code potentially memory-enhancing characteristics of therapeutic events were examined through the calculation of intraclass coefficients for interrater reliability, and correlational and factor analyses for relationships among the scales. The interrater reliability coefficients obtained were well within generally accepted ranges of reliability for rating scales used in therapeutic process research (.72 to .93), with the exception of some coefficients obtained for the "clarity" scale. This scale subsequently was dropped from further analyses. Our inspection of interscale correlations, and factors emerging from factor analyses of our data, led us to conclude that the scales of depth, elaboration, and conclusion orientation clearly measured related, but different, aspects of a single higher-order variable. (The variable, personalizing, appeared to be measuring something quite different.) In our view, an appropriate analogy, given the size and pattern of the correlations observed, was to tests of general intelligence made up of several distinct, but related, subscales. We speculated that the higher-order variable in this case might be something like "therapeutic experiencing" in the sense of focused exploration, interpretation, and restructuring of personal meanings and theories. Research by Sandra Paivio (1989) that has found high, positive correlations of our depth, elaboration, and conclusion-orientation scales with Klein's Experiencing Scales (Klein, Mathieu-Coughlan, & Kiesler, 1986) supports such an interpretation.

More substantively, results from analyses of differences between client-recalled important and control events on the variables of "depth of meaning," "elaboration of meaning through the use of figurative language, " and "conclusion orientation" of the therapeutic discourse revealed that these measures discriminated reliably and as predicted between the client-recalled and control events.

In addition, some limited support was obtained for a second hypothesis that "elaboration of meaning through the use of figurative language" would discriminate more reliably between client-recalled and control events during the experiential therapy sessions than during the cognitive therapy sessions. Finally, and of potentially significant clinical relevance, it was therapists' language (interactions) that contributed most to discriminations between client-recalled and control events on the depth, elaboration, and conclusion-orientation measures. Once more, the strong implication was that therapists could influence clients' encoding and recall of therapeutic conversations (discourse) through the nature of the language they employed during psychotherapy. However, we still lacked experimental evidence that such conversational effects on clients' episodic memory of therapy could be induced by a planned manipulation of characteristics of therapists' in-therapy language. We also had little evidence, at this stage, that such conversationally spawned episodic memories could mediate between therapeutic conversations and any therapeutically induced changes experienced by clients.

In a more recent study, we (Martin, Cummings, & Hallberg, 1992) conducted a direct test of therapists' intentional influence on clients' episodic encoding and recall of therapeutic conversations. Therapists in four dyads of experiential psychotherapy (7 to 13 sessions each) were trained to use therapeutic metaphors whenever they judged that such metaphoric interventions might promote legitimate, important client therapeutic work and were appropriate to the current therapeutic context. In essence, we asked therapists in this study to employ metaphoric interventions that they thought their clients would perceive as both relevant to, yet a bit (but not too) inconsistent with, their current understandings (personal theories). The rationale for selecting metaphoric communications as the experimental manipulation in this study was that such communications typically are rich in the sorts of elaborative, figurative language that has been shown to enhance memorability in both basic experimental (cf. Paivio, 1986) and applied therapeutic (e.g., Martin, Paivio, & Labadie, 1990; Martin & Stelmaczonek, 1988) contexts. Immediately after therapy sessions were completed, therapists and clients were asked to recall therapeutic events they found to be most memorable, and to give reasons for the memorability of these events. Participants also rated each session in terms of its helpfulness and effectiveness.

Specific hypotheses were: (1) that clients would tend to recall events associated with therapists' intentional metaphoric interventions, and (2) that clients would rate more positively sessions in which they recalled therapists' intentional metaphoric interventions than sessions in which they did not recall therapists' intentional metaphoric interventions. The rationale for the second hypothesis was the assumption that clients tend to recall therapeutic events when they have encoded them "deeply" in terms of the personal meanings and theories associated with them (cf. Craik & Tulving, 1975; Martin & Stelmaczonek, 1988). Thus, sessions during which therapists' intentional metaphorical interventions were recalled might contain more deep, meaningful elaboration of clients' meanings and theories than sessions during which therapists' intentional metaphoric interventions were not recalled. Consequently, such deep, meaningful elaboration and its presumed effects on recall of therapeutic conversations/events would seem to contribute significantly to clients' perceptions of session effectiveness and helpfulness.

In addition to the foregoing hypotheses, possible epistemic and motivational functions of metaphor use in therapy were examined by means of interpretive, natural-language analyses, following a more open-ended, discovery-oriented research strategy. Two research assistants and I independently examined clients' postsession, written accounts of their reasons for remembering the therapeutic events they recalled. We each attempted to describe these reasons in our own words. We then met to discuss our descriptions. These discussions led to a joint formulation of a small number of distinctive, epistemic and motivational functions about which we could reach comprehensive, consensual understanding.

Results were that clients recalled therapists' intentional use of metaphor in approximately two-thirds of the sessions in which metaphors were employed intentionally by therapists. Not surprisingly, metaphors that were recalled tended, almost without exception, to be developed and elaborated collaboratively and publicly through the active participation of both therapists and clients, and to be developed over considerable time, both within and across therapy sessions. With respect to clinical impact, clients rated sessions during which they recalled therapists' intentional metaphors as significantly more helpful than sessions during which they did not recall therapists' intentional metaphors. Similar results with respect to clients' ratings of session effectiveness just failed to reach statistical significance in the expected direction.

Results from the discovery-oriented, interpretive analyses suggested that therapists' intentional metaphors served two distinctive epistemic and two distinctive motivational functions. Epistemic effects noted were: (1) enhanced emotional awareness, and (2) conceptual "bridging," both of which may be seen as consistent with the notion of memory-mediated personal theory elaboration developed in this chapter. Motivational effects noted were: (1) enhanced relationship with therapist, and (2) goal clarification. It would seem that the process of memory-mediated personal theory revision, as triggered by therapists' intentional use of figurative language in therapeutic conversations, requires a sound working relationship between client and therapist in which therapeutic goals are clear and shared.

A few examples of therapists' use of metaphor to induce elaborations of clients' personal theories in the therapeutic conversations recalled by clients in the Martin, Cummings, and Hallberg (1992) study follow. The first quotation in each of the pairs is taken from an earlier portion of the therapeutic conversation than the second quotation in each pair. In considering these examples, it is important to note that the quotations are taken directly from transcriptions of therapists' statements during the psychotherapy sessions studied. These therapists' statements were identified through specific recollections (actual words, phrases, or extremely direct paraphrases) provided by clients in response to probes concerning memorable therapeutic events. The comments that appear in square brackets following these direct quotations help to place the quoted remarks in context.

"Like lemon juice being poured on an open wound." [In response to client's narration of her partner's reaction to her disclosure of illness.]

"Roses may be defective, yet still bloom." [In response to client's struggle to continue to develop and enjoy life, despite her illness and difficulties.]

"You've been crushed into moulds." [Topic is client's expression of feeling bullied by others.]

"It is difficult to cut them off, but remain connected to them." [Topic is changing relationships with others, so they will not be so influential in determining what the client should do and be.]

"It's a barrier that you can't break through." [Topic is client's partner's resistance to intimacy.]

"Behind your own wall, you too are vulnerable and hiding." [Topic is client's own resistance to intimacy.]

From these examples, taken from the therapy dyads studied by Martin and colleagues (1992), it is easy to imagine how the figurative language and metaphors employed by therapists in this study, and recalled by clients, might have fostered significant memory-mediated elaboration and revision of clients' problem-relevant, personal theories. Recalling the critical realist perspective on the testing of psychological theories, as developed in the latter part of chapter 1, the study by Martin and colleagues (1992) constitutes an ecologically valid, experimental verification test (warranted by semipredictive utility) of the ability of therapists intentionally to elaborate therapeutic conversations in ways that influence clients' episodic memories of such conversations.

Other Research

The general literature in therapeutic psychology is replete with clinical case studies and informal clinical observations concerning clients' memories of life experiences and the "working through," "revisiting," or "restructuring" of these memories as an important part of psychotherapeutic work (see Edwards, 1990, for a relatively recent review of these themes). In this work, the basic notion of using the psychotherapeutic conversation between therapist and client as a vehicle for the social, public elaboration of a client's experiential, episodic memories, and the personal theories explicitly and implicitly associated with them, finds external coherence. Recently, empirical case studies have begun to appear that document processes similar to the social, public, memory-mediated elaboration of clients' personal theories and belief systems that is posited herein.

Edwards (1990) reports case studies that support the clinical use of a therapeutic intervention in which guided imagery is employed to assist clients to recover and review "avoided" memories, identify the meanings/

beliefs associated with these memories and the emotions they encompass, and reevaluate such beliefs. In one of the case studies presented by Edwards, Richard (a 32-year-old attorney) suffering from depression and generalized anxiety is helped, through a process of guided imagery in the therapeutic conversation, to uncover memories of being scolded by his grandmother during his childhood. Psychodramatic elements introduced purposefully into the therapeutic conversation by the therapist gradually helped Richard to elaborate a personal theory that included propositions such as, "If the other person is angry, he must be right. If the other person is right, I must be wrong." After relevant episodic memories of his childhood also were elaborated, Richard was able to associate such simplistic, dichotomous propositions with his previous internalizations of his grandmother's scolding lectures: "I am the ultimate arbiter of right and wrong. If you do wrong, you are a bad person and are not acceptable to the family. If I am angry with you, it is because you have done wrong and are bad" (p. 40). Eventually he was able, with the aid of the therapist, to co-construct alternative, imagined conversations between himself, his mother, and his grandmother that helped him to understand that these internalized beliefs were attributable more to his grandmother's insensitivities, oversimplified worldviews, and overly zealous incorporation of these into her child-rearing practices than to fundamental shortcomings in himself. On the basis of such elaborations to his episodic memories and personal theories, Richard ceased to feel helpless and guilty when others in his current life (e.g., rival attorneys) were critical or confronting.

Other psychotherapy researchers have used case study and intensive methods to investigate possible relationships between forms and characteristics of therapeutic discourse/conversation and the elaboration of clients' episodic memories and personal theories in psychotherapy, especially those memorial and theoretical elements that are tacit, repressed, affectively laden, and experiential. For example, Price and Bucci (1989) have shown how the use of concrete, vivid, specific, and clear language can encourage client referential activity and subsequent verbalization of previously repressed memories. This work has involved detailed linguistic analyses of therapeutic conversations. For example, psychoanalytic interpretations offered by the therapist were characterized as successful in encouraging client referential activity if subsequent client contributions to the therapeutic conversation included heretofore absent "reports of actions and emotions, experiences of them in the session itself, or descriptions of images, fantasies, and dreams in concrete and specific terms" (Bucci, 1985, p. 602).

Still other researchers have studied the manner in which figurative, metaphoric language in therapeutic conversations can help clients to elaborate their affective experiences more fully and to integrate these elaborations into extended systems of personal understanding. Small-N studies by Angus and Rennie (1988, 1989), McMullen (1985, 1989), and Pollio and Barlow (1975) have employed mostly qualitative, discovery-oriented methodologies to yield a wealth of suggestive, ecologically valid information of this sort. For example, Angus and Rennie (1988) studied the collaborative co-construction of metaphors in therapeutic conversations. They identified characteristics of such conversations that led to the development of mutually shared understandings of the clients' personal theories versus the development of joint misunderstandings of the clients' meanings and theories. This work indicates that the various conversational elements frequently associated with the therapeutic elaboration of clients' episodic memories and personal theories (e.g., imagery, metaphor, concrete language, and so forth) do not automatically ensure therapeutic success. Obviously, a great deal depends on enabling factors such as the overall quality of the relationship between a client and a therapist, the client's current capabilities and levels of functioning, and the therapist's ability to comprehend, and communicate in a manner consistent with, the client's theoretical and experiential framework (see Muran & DiGiuseppe, 1990, for a critical consideration of such topics). In the theoretical formulations considered earlier in this chapter, factors such as perceived relevance and mild inconsistency, operating at the interface of clients' personal theories and therapists' contributions to the therapeutic conversation, are believed to be especially important. However, overall, there is considerable evidence to indicate that the use of concrete, figurative language and metaphor in therapeutic conversations can foster therapeutically productive elaborations of clients' personal theories in the social forum of psychotherapy and that such elaborations frequently are mediated by clients' episodic recollections of past and extratherapeutic experiences (see also Gonçalves & Craine, 1990). [The critical realist position described in chapter 1 allows the postulation of a causal mechanism through which such discourse vehicles potentially can influence elaborations and revisions to clients' personal theories, even though these discourse vehicles and such theoretical shifts may not be consistently or definitively correlated in real-world psychotherapeutic contexts. In critical realism, claims concerning possible generative, causal mechanisms are not confused with correlative, statistical observations or claims. Critical realism rejects the Humean causal account adopted by positivist and empiricist philosophies of science and social science, which equates observed, descriptive associations with causal explanations (cf. Greenwood, 1989).]

While other researchers of psychotherapy have studied topics relevant to the memory-mediated elaboration of clients' personal theories in psychotherapy, there has been little empirical work, other than that conducted by me and my colleagues, that has attempted to study the memory-mediated revision of clients' personal theories as a result of their encoding and extratherapeutic recollection of events and episodes from psychotherapeutic interactions and conversations per se. Hopefully, more work of this sort will occur in the future. In the meantime, the basic notion that clients' episodic memories of psychotherapeutic conversations enable them to retain and incorporate new understandings into their personal, private theories (which have been elaborated in the social, public arena of psychotherapy) in ways that permit and support more functional actions in relevant extratherapeutic contexts has considerable face validity. It also receives initial support from our own program of research, as summarized in the immediately preceding section of this chapter. Additional support from theory-driven, case study research will be discussed in the next chapter.

THEORETICAL COHERENCE

The relevance of memories of life experiences to psychotherapy and therapeutic change has long been recognized. Indeed, it seems impossible to understand how psychotherapy possibly might connect to clients' everyday, extratherapeutic experiences without making use of clients' memories of episodes in their past and current daily lives. In this chapter, I have proposed several major theoretical propositions that elaborate and refine this core idea, within the neo-Vygotskian template articulated in chapters 1 and 2.

1. Clients' episodic memories of past and current life events and conversations enable them to discuss their life experiences in the psychotherapeutic context.
2. Specific, identifiable features of the co-constructed therapeutic conversation between therapists and clients enable greater verbal elaboration of the extratherapeutic episodic memories of clients, together with the personal theories (personalized systems of beliefs and knowledge) associated with them.
3. Many of these same conversational characteristics, together with "interface" characteristics such as relevance and mild inconsistency, enhance the memorability of episodes in the therapeutic conversation itself.

4. Clients' episodic memories of psychotherapy enable them to retain aspects of therapeutic elaborations of their past memories and personal theories.

5. These therapeutic memories, in interaction with current and future life experiences, enable clients to revise personal theories that are relevant to their concerns and problems, eventually resulting in personal theories capable of supporting thoughts and actions that will enable clients to resolve or cope more successfully with their life circumstances.

These propositions constitute the core claims in the theory of therapeutic change with which this book is concerned. Propositions 1 and 2 describe the mediational role of clients' episodic memories of past and current extratherapeutic experiences and conversations in the social, public elaboration of their personal theories during psychotherapy. Propositions 3, 4, and 5 describe the mediational role of clients' episodic memories of psychotherapeutic experiences and conversations in the private, cognitive revision of their personal theories. In this formulation of therapeutic change, clients' episodic memories are the basic psychological tools that enable clients to articulate and elaborate their internalizations of previous life experiences and conversations, and then to reinternalize significant aspects of the now more elaborated, articulated personal theories that emerge from these therapeutic conversations. Psychotherapy is a unique form of conversation that attempts to alter the personal theories about themselves, others, and life circumstances that clients have internalized from their participation in other (previous and ongoing) intimate, social, and cultural conversations. Episodic memory is the basic mediational mechanism or psychological tool that enables this therapeutic change process.

What is unique about this formulation of the role of episodic memory in therapeutic change is not the long-recognized relevance of clients' memories to psychotherapy, but a more detailed explanation of exactly how clients' memories might function to mediate critical processes of personal theory elaboration and revision within a relatively nondualistic, social psychological framework. It is the specific mediational roles I have postulated for clients' episodic memories in fostering therapeutic change, and the close interfacing of these memories with characteristics of therapeutic and extratherapeutic conversations, that are unique to the theory I am presenting. Once the nature and functions of clients' episodic memories with respect to therapeutic change have been articulated, it is possible to interpret existing theoretical formulations of therapeutic change in more precise and complete ways. With these ideas in mind, earlier, more general and vague theoretical formulations of the role of memory in therapeutic work take on new precision and meaning.

For example, as early as 1914, Freud (1914/1966) described therapeutic phenomena closely related to the notion of memory mediation of personal theory elaboration as developed earlier in this chapter.

> Forgetting impressions, scenes or experiences nearly always reduces itself to shutting them off. When the patient talks about these "forgotten" things he seldom fails to add: "As a matter of fact, I've always known it; only I've never thought of it." (p. 148)

The therapeutic elaboration of nonverbal, experiential, imaginal episodic memories, and associated personal theories, as developed herein (following Tulving, Paivio, and Bucci) provides an informative theoretical context in which Freud's descriptions of such important therapeutic phenomena can be understood.

Another example of how the current theoretical formulation enables a coherent explication of previous, significant formulations of therapeutic change is found in relation to Liotti's (1986) explication of the joint functions of therapeutic elaboration and revision of clients' personal theories (in Liotti's terms, "representational models").

> The relationship between episodic memories of early experiences, explicit self-descriptions and ongoing evaluation of emotional and interpersonal occurrences should be repeatedly stressed. The old structure of memory, self-concept and peripheral cognition should then be contrasted with alternative and more adaptive representational models, to be envisaged both by the patient and the therapist. Only after this process has been gone through many times are the revised models likely to be stable. (p. 114)

In this brief excerpt from his work, Liotti clearly envisions a theoretical formulation of therapeutic change quite compatible with the current formulation. However, in Liotti's work there is little articulation of the role of episodic memories of therapeutic conversations in mediating between these conversations and clients' personal theory revisions in extratherapeutic contexts. Nonetheless, the general coherence of the set of theoretical propositions developed in this chapter with such past formulations is important testimony to the concurrent validity of the present formulations. That the five propositions stated at the beginning of this section of the chapter may be seen to extend and elaborate such previous theoretical frameworks indicates an important form of progressive theoretical development.

It clearly is impossible to reference all previous work that might be interpreted as coherent with the ideas of memory-mediation of personal theory elaboration and revision that I have presented. Once again, work on memory and the revision or restructuring of memories and personal theories (worldviews, representational structures or models, schemas, belief systems) is ubiquitous in the general psychotherapeutic literature. Other recent attempts to develop more precise formulations of the roles of personal memories and theories in therapeutic change with which I am familiar include those by Bowlby (1985), Bonanno (1990), Liotti (1986), Mahoney (1990), and Toukmanian (1992). In addition, potentially useful discussions of memories that seem to be shared collectively by many individuals with similar social-cultural and experiential backgrounds can be found in Connerton (1989) and Middleton and Edwards (1990). These latter works may hold unique value for theorizing about processes of memory-mediated change in various approaches to group and family psychotherapy.

Many of the conceptualizations I have presented in this chapter, and the phenomena to which they relate, are extremely well established in current and extant work on psychotherapy and therapeutic change. It is the overall theoretical integration of these conceptualizations into a less dualistic, testable account of therapeutic change that constitutes the uniqueness, and hopefully the value, of this book. This chapter's articulation of the potential richness and utility of Tulving's and Paivio's conceptualizations of human episodic memory with respect to psychotherapeutic change is an extremely important component of this work. In the words of Proust (1924), "the quality of a direct experience always eludes one and that only in recollection can we grasp its real flavor" (p. vii).

Chapter 4

THEORIES

A theory provides a basis for an active approach to life, not
merely a comfortable armchair from which to contemplate
its vicissitudes with detached complaisance. (G. Kelly,
1955, pp. 18–19)

Generally speaking, scientific theories are collections of propositions through which there is an attempt to explain some phenomenon of
interest. Collections of propositions about X are considered a theory
about X if they are constructed in such a manner that the terms they
contain gain their meaning through their systemic relations or through
connections to observations. Different philosophies of science place differing interpretations on the nature of the relationships assumed to hold
between theories and the phenomena they attempt to explain. Some
forms of positivism and operationalism assume that observed associations of focal phenomena constitute an adequate theory of these phenomena. Various forms of relativism emphasize systemic relations internal to a theory itself and essentially ignore observational links. Still other
philosophies of science, such as pragmatism and critical realism, assume
that systemic, metaphysical relations in a theory can be tested by observations that are not entailed by the theory and should cohere to other
relevant theories external to the theory itself.

Philosophies of science also differ with respect to what constitutes
explanation: causal explanation warranted by predictive utility, elaborative description warranted by enriched meaning and plausibility, narrative understanding warranted by personal resonance, and so forth. Despite philosophical differences in their construal, scientific theories must
meet social/public criteria that are established by scientists working
within particular paradigms and communities. Further, within these par-

adigmatic/community conventions, scientific theories must be perceived as explaining focal phenomena in some acceptable manner.

In personal theories, there also is an attempt to explain phenomena of interest, but typically in a much less formal, less public, more tacit, and less constrained manner. In the most general sense, a personal theory about X refers to an individual's construals of, or beliefs about, X. This personal knowledge may be inconsistent with more public, consensual knowledge about X, but may constitute a private, personal explanation (in the sense of "understanding") of X. Despite obvious differences in the nature and warranting of scientific and personal theories, many psychologists hold that all theories, personal or scientific, function to permit individuals who hold them to make sense of, and determine courses of action in relation to, relevant phenomenal contexts. From this perspective, it may be that the ways in which individuals develop and use personal theories in their everyday lives, are somewhat akin to the ways in which scientists develop and test more formal theories.

The theory of therapeutic change being presented in this book emphasizes the internalization (via the mediation of personal episodic memories) of intimate, social, and cultural conversations (including the practical activities associated with them) into the personal theories of clients. It holds that therapeutic conversations are special forms of conversation that attempt to elaborate and revise the personal theories that clients have internalized from previous dialogical experiences, but which currently do not permit them to achieve desired goals or to resolve or cope with difficulties in their lives. Given the centrality of personal theories to this formulation of therapeutic change, an explication of such theories, and a more extended discussion of their elaboration and revision, is warranted. In this chapter, relevant work by George Kelly (1955) is presented, and then modified and extended through a consideration of related work by Rom Harré (1984), Charles Taylor (1989, 1991), Hazel Markus (1983, Markus & Nurius, 1986), and others. These discussions lead into a more specific formulation of the revision and elaboration of clients' personal theories in psychotherapy. The chapter ends with a discussion of empirical and conceptual work that supports and tests various aspects of this formulation.

KELLY'S PSYCHOLOGY OF PERSONAL CONSTRUCTS

The possibility that personal theories might perform functions for the individuals holding them that are somewhat analogous to the functions that scientific theories perform for communities of scientists finds exacting expression in the work of George Kelly (1955). Just as scientific theories are developed to help scientists anticipate, explain, predict, and control phenomena of interest, personal theories are developed to assist individuals in anticipating, understanding, and acting upon occurrences in their own lives. The metaphor of *person as scientist* is central to Kelly's work. For Kelly, purposeful human change inevitably involves an investigation into the personal construct or theoretical system of the individual seeking change.

The basis of Kelly's ideas and proposals concerning human change is his theory of *personal constructs.* This theory is expressed in his 1955 book, *A Theory of Personality: The Psychology of Personal Constructs,* in formal statements of one fundamental postulate, together with 11 accompanying corollaries. In a manner of presentation that seems intended to promote empirical testing of his claims, Kelly (1955) states his fundamental postulate as follows: "A person's processes are psychologically channelized by the ways in which he anticipates events" (p. 45). Precise definitions of each of the terms that appear in this postulate leave little doubt that in making this claim Kelly commits himself to a psychological position that considers humans to act holistically (motivationally, cognitively, affectively, and behaviorally) on the basis of their construals (theories) of themselves and the events they experience. As Neimeyer (1986) explains,

> he [Kelly] took persons and their processes as the central concern of this theory, and built in the anticipation of the future as its primary motivational principle. Thus, from the outset, he made clear that it was human beings in their entirety that he was discussing, not lower organisms or "parts" of persons considered in isolation (e.g., their "cognition"). Furthermore, by concerning himself with the way our ongoing processes are channelled, he bypassed the need to devise explanations for why an "inert" organism would become active in the first place, thereby discarding unnecessary concepts such as libidinal energy, drives, motives, and stimuli. Instead he assumed that the person is essentially a "form of motion," and that the direction we take with our lives depends upon the constructs we employ for anticipating our futures. (p. 229)

Kelly's elaboration of his fundamental postulate through formal statements of 11 corollaries may be summarized in terms of his claims about (1) the *process of construing,* (2) the *structural features of personal construct systems,* and (3) the *social-embeddedness of personal construct systems* (I follow Neimeyer, 1986, here). My use of the terms *personal theory* and *personal theorizing* essentially equates with Kelly's use of the terms *personal construct system* and *personal construing,* with exceptions to be noted.

Process of Construing

With respect to the process of construing or personal theorizing, Kelly holds that this process consists most basically of discerning recurrent regularities or themes in one's experiences that can be used to anticipate related experiences in the future. As informal scientists, we make implicit predictions that we then invest in actions (experiments). These actions yield experiential evidence that supports or invalidates our anticipations, resulting in experientially induced revisions to our systems of personal constructs on which our predictions are based. As a consequence of our ongoing experiences, we progressively revise our construct systems, hoping to enhance their predictive and explanatory utility.

However, like all theories, personal theories have both advantages and disadvantages. The more rigorously held our theories are, the more impermeable they may become to experiences that are not consistent with them. When this happens, experiential results of our actions may be distorted or ignored, rather than used as a basis for productive theory revision. This particular aspect of Kelly's theory of personal constructs is quite similar to Rogerian and other humanistic, experiential theories of human change that view rigidity in the individual as restricting opportunities for optimal experiential development and self-actualization. However, Kelly's theory has a concreteness and a concern for explanation (beyond a general understanding) of human experience that is somewhat at odds with many of the values held by more humanistic theorists (see Jankowicz, 1987). At the same time, Kelly's emphasis on the whole person (i.e., his refusal to separate cognitive from motivational and affective phenomena) is distinct from many cognitive, information processing accounts of human change that emphasize alterations to mental schemata or structures (see Ingram, 1986). As some have argued (cf. Davisson, 1978), the foregoing differences from mainstream Western psychologies may have retarded wide dissemination of Kelly's ideas, especially in the 1960s and 1970s.

Structural Features of Personal Construct Systems

Most obviously unique to Kelly's (1955) formulations is the way in which he conceptualized personal constructs and systems of personal constructs. Psychology, since its mainstream conversion to cognitivism in the past 4 decades, has developed numerous terms to connote the representation and organization of mental content. Most such terms (including *cognitive structures, conceptual schemata, knowledge networks,* and so forth) are formulated in terms of concepts and their propositional interconnections, arranged hierarchically according to progressively greater levels of abstraction (cf. Ashcraft, 1989).

In addition to his refusal to equate personal constructs with cognitive structures alone, Kelly postulated a dialectical quality to his basic conceptual unit, the personal construct. His *dichotomy corollary* states that "a person's construction system is composed of a finite number of dichotomous constructs" (p. 59). Kelly believed that personal meanings are essentially attained through contrast. He represented this core idea by proposing a bipolar structure for each individual construct dimension. Thus, for example, a client in psychotherapy who is experiencing difficulties in maintaining friendships might organize experiences in terms of a personal construct dimension defined at opposite poles as "supportive" versus "disruptive." Assuming that this construct dimension is central to this client's construct system, the client's functional use of such a construct in anticipating and participating in interpersonal interactions in everyday life might translate into a quick appraisal of the actions of others as supportive or disruptive to the client's own concerns and activities. This initial assessment then might be followed by a premature decision to sustain or interrupt interpersonal contacts accordingly.

The bipolar character of Kelly's personal constructs suggests that personal theories are, at least in part, structured dichotomously. Potentially important therapeutic implications of this dichotomy corollary are that clients who have utilized one end of a core personal construct more than the other nonetheless possess dialectical capability for elaborating the heretofore underdeveloped side of this construct dimension, should they decide to do so. Thus, many gestalt and psychodramatic methods in psychotherapy that attempt to utilize clients' dialectical capabilities to elaborate their personal awareness and understanding, may derive support from Kelly's theory (cf. Greenberg, 1984).

At a more macroscopic level of system structure, Kelly (1955) envisions a multilevel organization of ordinal relationships among the various constructs in a personal construct system, "with some constructs subsuming others and those, in turn, subsuming still others" (p. 57). For example, the client who construes interpersonal interactions as supportive or disruptive may represent meanings for each pole in this construct dimension in terms of various poles in a variety of other construct dimensions. Thus, "supportive" may derive meaning from "loving" and "concerned" poles of construct dimensions of "loving–hateful" and "concerned–irresponsible." On the other hand, the entire "supportive–disruptive" construct may enter into the personal meaning given to the "evaluative" pole of a more abstracted, procedural construct dimension of "evaluative–descriptive." Thus, this same client may believe that it is possible to evaluate social interactions using dimensions such as "supportive" and "disruptive," rather than simply perceiving and noting them. The valuing of focal phenomena that inevitably is built into any system of personal constructs provides a motivational basis for construing and behaving, one that is inseparable from the basic epistemic structure of the entire system of personal constructs.

It also is worth mentioning that an individual may employ a variety of construct subsystems that may be incompatible with each other, depending on the nature of existing relationships between different constructs or clusters of constructs. This *fragmentation corollary* helps to explain why a client might interpret the same action by different individuals as supportive in one case and disruptive in another. If past experiences have led to conflicting appraisals of these individuals in terms of their "goodness–badness" or "trustworthiness–suspiciousness," different subsystems of personal constructs may be employed in interacting with these different people, even though these subsystems may be inferentially incompatible with each other.

In general, the more superordinate and abstract a construct (i.e., the more cross-referenced with more concrete, subordinate construct dimensions), the more stable and resistant to change it is. This is especially true when abstract, superordinate constructs bear directly on one's self-identity. For example, a client who somehow equates self-worth with others' positive attention is likely to overuse a personal construct dimension such as "supportive–disruptive" in anticipating and interpreting the social responses of others. The consequence of such overuse might be a failure to benefit from unsupportive feedback when the client's own actions have warranted such responses.

Neimeyer (1986) has drawn comparisons between Kelly's structural assumptions and their implications for psychotherapeutic change, and the work of Guidano and Liotti (1983, 1985; Liotti, 1986) in adapting Lakatos' (1970) theory of scientific change to a structural theory of personal change in psychotherapy. This conceptual link serves to associate directly Kelly's theory of personal constructs with theory elaboration and revision in both scientific and therapeutic contexts. Consequently, it is directly relevant to the conceptualization of personal theory revision in psychotherapy that is the focal concern in this chapter.

Lakatos (1970, 1978) suggested that scientific research programs consist of a succession of theories linked by a common "hard core" of shared commitments. A "protective belt" of dispensable hypotheses wards off direct empirical assault on this core. The hard core of a scientific research program is a set of basic assumptions (propositions) that is the source of the central hypotheses on which the entire program is based. An example of such a hypothesis is the central belief of radical behaviorists that human behavior is conditioned by its consequences, unmediated in any causal manner by "inner mental" events.

Scientists working in a research program develop a series of auxiliary hypotheses that derives from the hard core assumptions. According to Lakatos, the functional effect, although most often not the consciously intended effect, of these auxiliary hypotheses (i.e., the "protective belt") is to protect the core assumptions and hypotheses from critical tests or conceptual critiques that might destroy them. Thus, for example, countless studies have been conducted within the radical behavioral research program in psychology and psychotherapy that have compared and analyzed how and how well different operant conditioning schedules, contingencies, and interventions produce the effects that researchers attribute to them. These same researchers, however, have steered away from empirical and conceptual tests of the central idea of unmediated, situational causality. Whenever demonstrations have been provided of how such critical tests might be undertaken, they have come from researchers working outside of the radical behavioral program (e.g., Howard & Conway, 1986). However, eventually such tests, and associated conceptual developments, may lead to the relative abandonment of one research program (in this example, the radical behavioral program) in favor of a seemingly more progressive research program (such as the currently popular cognitive research program in psychology).

As stated earlier, the potential relationship between Lakatos's conceptualization of the progressive revision of scientific theories and the psychotherapeutically induced revision of clients' personal theories has been elaborated by Guidano and Liotti (1983, 1985; Liotti, 1986). These theorists of psychotherapeutic change explicitly modeled their conceptualization of the structure of personal theories after the structure of scientific research programs developed by Lakatos. They identified three levels in an individual's cognitive organization that correspond to Lakatos's levels of metaphysical hard core, protective belt, and actual research plans.

The *core* level of an individual's cognitive, theoretical organization comprises schemata that are formed during childhood and adolescence and are tacitly held by the individual as unquestionable assumptions about important aspects of self and reality. The *intermediate* level of an individual's cognitive, theoretical organization consists of "protective," verbalizable descriptions of oneself, other people, and the world. Here, Liotti (1986, p. 98) stresses the polarized, dichotomous character of these constructions and explicitly relates them to Kelly's conceptualization of personal constructs. Of further relevance to the theoretical formulations he sets forth, Liotti (1986) states that "the relationship between the explicit descriptions of the intermediate level and the core emotional schemata is akin to that between semantic memory and episodic memory" (p. 98), citing Tulving as a source for this latter distinction. At any rate, the explicit descriptions of the intermediate level function to protect the core assumptions an individual holds about self and reality.

Finally, the *peripheral* level of individual cognitive, theoretical organization encompasses the plans of action and the problem-solving strategies an individual uses to navigate the demands of daily life. Appraisals, evaluations, interpretations, and reactions to daily events, while arising from a multilevel interaction between these events and all three levels of an individual's cognitive, theoretical organization, are manifest at this level.

Liotti (1986) illustrated his theory with an example of a client suffering from severe agoraphobia. According to Liotti, this client's daily plans of action ("research plans") involved avoidance of situations away from places of safety or trustworthy persons and avoidance of situations from which he could not readily escape (e.g., crowded public places such as buses or trains). The "protective belt" of intermediate constructs adopted by this client centered around a polarized view of himself as "ill" and therefore unable to control his reactions and behavior. As Liotti's therapeutic interventions revealed, however, the "hard core" of personal, emotional schemata being shielded by this protective self-description included a set of core beliefs acquired early in the client's developmental history. These beliefs concerned the importance of being a "real man" and "maintaining absolute self-control at all costs." Consequently, whenever his absolute control of events was threatened by current circumstances, the client began to reassert control by resorting to agoraphobic responses, rationalizing this pattern of behavior as that of a person who is "ill" rather than "weak" or "out-of-control."

It is particularly interesting to note how, during Liotti's work with this client in psychotherapy, the client's eventual recovery was facilitated by an elaboration of his theory of his illness to include episodic recollections about "the ways in which he learnt to control 'womanish' emotions, and discovered how these ways were connected to fearful images of loneliness, to oppressive experiences of reduced personal freedom, and to paternal injunctions of 'machismo'" (p. 122). Eventually, such elaborations yielded significant revisions to the client's personal cognitive, theoretical organization at all three levels, as he came gradually to "understand how self-control prevented him from trying to understand his own emotions" (p. 122). A major consequence of this process of theory elaboration and revision was that the client eventually was able to give up polarized self-descriptions and other-descriptions at the intermediate level. These polarized descriptions had limited his exploration of his own experiences, and his self-expression in intimate relationships, to understandings and actions congruent with his culturally and socially induced conception of himself as a strong man. As his acceptance of his "weaker" emotions and experiences expanded, he was able to acknowledge and accept his previously troubling reactions to current work and marital circumstances as legitimate and no longer sought to avoid them through agoraphobic behavior.

Social-Embeddedness of Personal Construct Systems

A final group of corollaries stated by Kelly (1955) emphasizes the importance of social context in individuals' constructions of reality through their systems of personal constructs. Although Kelly held, in his *individuality corollary,* that people "differ from each other in their construction of events" (p. 55), he recognized that such personal uniqueness must somehow be constrained by the social and cultural realities in which individuals reside. Otherwise, meaningful interpersonal interaction would be impossible. It is Kelly's articulation of the social-embeddedness of personal construct systems that makes it possible to integrate aspects of his theory of personal constructs with the sort of neo-Vygotskian template articulated in chapter 2. Two of Kelly's corollaries speak directly to this issue.

In his *commonality corollary,* he states that "to the extent that one person employs a construction of experience which is similar to that employed by another, his psychological processes are similar to those of the other person" (p. 90). In this statement, Kelly implicitly recognizes that individuals' constructions and anticipations of events in their lives may have similarities that stem from similar psychological processes. The actual source of such psychological similarities is made clear in his discussion extending this corollary.

> People belong to the same cultural group, not merely because they behave alike, nor because they expect the same things of others, but especially because they construe their experience in the same way. It is on this last similarity that the psychology of personal constructs throws its emphasis. (p. 94)

It would be a mistake to imply that in making statements such as this Kelly was moving away from a psychological emphasis on individual experience. Rather, he seems to be acknowledging a sort of functional interrelationship between social-cultural context and psychological processes and experience. The way in which shared psychological processes and experience, presumably arising from shared social-cultural context, facilitate social interaction, is the topic of his final corollary, the *sociality corollary*. Here, he states, "To the extent that one person construes the construction processes of another, he may play a role in a social process involving the other person" (p. 95). In elaborating this statement, Kelly urges psychotherapists to work collaboratively with clients to explicate clients' construction systems. He advocates roleplays, experiments, and critical reflection as means of altering clients' systems of personal constructs in ways that might assist clients to be more adept at anticipating and interpreting events in their extratherapeutic experiences.

Kelly's theory of personal constructs provides an initial basis for considering the nature of clients' personal theories and their revision through psychotherapeutic conversations. However, though recognizing the social-embeddedness of personal theories and their therapeutic revision, Kelly's position is essentially dualistic. He consistently emphasizes the primacy of individuals' constructions of self and reality, even while describing the process of psychotherapy as one in which socially embedded, public discussions of clients' construct systems (personal theories) might facilitate functional revisions to those systems. Consequently, Kelly's formulations of the revision of personal theories are not adequate for a less dualistic account of therapeutic change, such as that attempted here. The works of Rom Harré (1984), Charles Taylor (1989, 1991), and Hazel Markus (1983; Markus & Nurius, 1986) help to elaborate some of Kelly's important contributions in a direction more directly amenable to the template for human change adopted herein (see chapters 1 and 2).

HARRÉ'S THEORY OF PERSONAL BEING

In chapter 2, Harré's (1984) work was used to elaborate Vygotsky's analysis of the interrelationships between cultural conversations and individuals' psychological processes and personal theories. The result was a more agenic, creative conception of personal being than seems to be envisioned in Vygotsky's work alone. Here, Harré's work is used to fashion a more socially constrained, less individualistic perspective on personal experiencing and theorizing than might be obtained from Kelly's work alone. In both cases, Harré's conceptualization of personal development as the acquisition and elaboration of a theory of self that is heavily, although not totally, constrained by social, cultural, and historical contexts helps to maintain a balance between social and personal causation by emphasizing the social–personal interface.

In chapter 2, I summarized Harré's theory of human development. It will be recalled that this theory posits four stages of development: (1) an *appropriation* stage in which the individual internalizes public, social, and cultural forms; (2) a *transformation* stage during which the individual uses these internalized forms as psychological tools to organize ongoing experiences; (3) a *publication* stage during which the individual expresses the products of private, transformational processes in the public, social arena; and (4) a *conventionalization* stage during which publicly displayed, individually realized psychological products become accepted into the shared knowledge and conventions of one's society and culture. Through this theory, Harré attempts to frame a nondualistic explanation of how collective, public forms (of perceiving, understanding, knowing, believing, feeling, relating, and so forth) become internalized as individual, private forms that persons can transform through their own experiences. Once transformed, such individual, private forms are subsequently displayed (published) and may be incorporated into collective, public forms. For Harré, the development of persons begins with the social/collective and returns to the social/collective. Nonetheless, the fact that each individual has the potential to make unique contributions to social, collective forms as a consequence of transformational processes grounded in unique personal, experiential histories enables a nondualistic conception of *human agency* (i.e., the capacity of persons to contribute novel input to social, collective forms).

Of critical importance to Harré's theory of agency in personal development is his construal of *self* as a theory that an individual holds about the "me" in personal experiences. During the transformational stage of development, the very nature of an individual's experience in the world is altered. Whereas previously the developing individual was internalizing public, collective conversations and associated activities, the individual now uses these internalized forms to begin to structure her or his own experiences. Particular events become instantiated with personal, private forms of understanding, engendering a distinctive, autobiographical self-consciousness. Through transformation, individuals become able to organize experiences as their own. Central to this ability to develop implicit, and eventually explicit, theories of one's experiences is the formation of a theory of self. As Harré states, "Our personal being is created by our coming to believe a theory of self based on our society's working conception of a person" (p. 26).

While Harré views *person* as an empirical concept that distinguishes an individual in the public, collective realm, he understands *self* as a theory of the personal unity an individual takes himself or herself to be. He actually proposes three fundamental unities that enter into an individual's framing of self as a theory held about "me": (1) point of view, (2) point of action, and (3) life trajectory. Other unities that enter into an individual's theory of self arise out of these basic unities of experience and include identity, consciousness, and agency, together with their respective, reflexive forms of autobiography, self-consciousness, and self-mastery. In Harré's (1984) words,

> when we learn to organize our organically grounded experience as a structured field, and cognitively as a body of beliefs built up of self-predications, we are deploying a concept of "self" that functions like the deep theoretical concepts of the natural sciences, which serve to organize our experience and knowledge, whether or not they have observable referents in the real world. (p. 145)

In all of this, it is important to note that self as a theory arises out of experience in the social, collective world, not from the unfolding of some preexisting set of biological mechanisms awaiting experiential triggers or from some set of Platonic or Kantian preexisting categories of mind. Once a theory of self (or, more accurately, "self as a theory") is in place, other personal theories of one's experiences in the world become possible. These are articulated implicitly and explicitly through the developmental processes of transformation and publication, as envisioned by Harré.

For the present purposes, the importance of Harré's explanation of personal development (which treats self and related beliefs and knowledge as personal theories that arise from one's experience in the public, collective world) is that it enables an understanding of how personal theories (such as Kelly's systems of personal constructs) might arise developmentally from participation in social, collective conversations. When psychotherapy is viewed as a special form of conversation aimed at the elaboration and revision of the personal theories individuals hold as a result of their developmental histories (and their episodic memories of these personal histories), such an explanation helps to formulate a more complete theory of therapeutic change, one that is fully contextualized in the life experiences of clients. If personal theories (including core theories of self, others, and the world) really do arise from participation in public, collective conversations, it is easier to conceive of psychotherapy as a form of "corrective" conversation that conceivably might lead to the public elaboration and private revision of those personal theories of clients that lie at the heart of their current difficulties and concerns. Harré's (1984) emphasis on self as a theory derivative from experiences in the social, public arena may be construed as compatible with a notion developed in the previous chapter, that "self" may be a theoretically organized aggregation of experiential, autobiographical memories. However, to make such an interpretation coherent, it is necessary to go beyond the radical, neo-Wittgensteinian monism (antimentalism) that pervades much of Harré's work.

TAYLOR'S DIALOGICAL SELF

The work of Charles Taylor (1989, 1991, 1992) permits the maintenance of a generally nondualistic account of self-development, but one that still allows for a more transcendental conception of self. Harré's "self as a theory" is a very particular kind of transcendental entity comprising the unities of point of view, point of action, and life trajectory. These are not especially malleable. Further, while they capture the "me" in human experience, they do not provide a genuine sense of the "I" as an agenic source experienced in a human life. Consequently, Harré's work on self (as opposed to his theory of personal development) is somewhat limited in its direct relevance to a theory of psychotherapeutic change.

As discussed in chapter 2, Taylor also endorses a social-cultural perspective on self-development that emphasizes the internalization of entire utterances in conversations. In particular, Taylor suggests that we see ourselves as "selves" because we identify with *morally* important self-descriptions we encounter in our dialogical experiences in the world, descriptions that locate us relative to standards of "the good," "the excellent," "the just," and so forth. To have a self-identity is to know where we stand on questions of value and issues of importance. Our sense of self situates us in ethical, not just social-cultural and personal space.

As with all of our understandings according to Taylor, various aspects of our conceptions of self are both represented in our minds and situated in our practices. Self-understanding is essentially dialogical (see chapter 2). While "the 'I' appears in our experience in memory" (Mead, 1934/1974, p. 196), it continuously and dynamically unfolds in the context of an ongoing internalized dialogue.

> The conversation between the "I" and the "me," or between one's own self-generated transformation of the offered scenarios and their

original form, is not between an introjected identity and some un-
formed principle of spontaneity. It is more a matter of gradually finding one's own voice as an interlocutor, realizing a possibility that was
inscribed in the original situation of dependence [i.e., dependence of a
child on parents and elders] in virtue of its dialogical form. (Taylor,
1991, p. 313)

Thus, Taylor's view of self-development is that an agenic sense of
the "I" in human life unfolds in an ethical space created through dialogical experience, both as originally encountered and as internalized, recollected, and transformed. Taylor's account permits a conception of self
with socially constituted origins, but with the possibility of transcending
those origins with the experience of additional conversations containing
alternative dialogical possibilities. [In closing this brief recapitulation of
some of Taylor's views, I should note that Taylor (1989) is far from
complementary to psychotherapeutic practices that embrace detached
forms of subjectivism and assume that significant human development
and change can occur in the absence of a well-developed moral sense of
what is "good" and "virtuous" in human life. In using some of Taylor's
views to support my own preferred version of a socially constituted, yet
transcendent self, I have not placed similar emphasis on moral development per se. At the same time, I have considerable sympathy for Taylor's
sense of moral imperative.]

MARKUS'S THEORY OF POSSIBLE SELVES

A final issue that demands resolution, if the current theory of psychotherapeutic change as a conversationally induced, memory-mediated
process of personal theory revision, is to be convincing, concerns the
possible sources of an individual's theoretical revisions. Clearly, psychotherapists must, as Kelly noted, come to understand clients' existing
personal theories. As these theories are discussed in psychotherapy, they
may be elaborated in ways that promote altered understandings and
actions. But, what is the foundation on which potentially functional
elaborations to clients' personal theories might be built?

In chapter 3, discussion focused on the elaboration of clients' personal theories that might arise from the therapeutic "unfolding" of tacit,
repressed, or implicit aspects of personal theories contained in heretofore
nonverbalizable episodic memories of past extratherapeutic experiences.
However, if the sole source for the therapeutic elaboration of clients'
personal theories resides in clients' existing theories (including previously

tacit, implicit elements), it is difficult to understand how clients might be helped to elaborate and acquire significantly new theoretical forms, different from their previously and currently held theories. Some sort of "immaculate theoretical conception" seems necessary, yet extremely difficult to comprehend.

One obvious line of response to this issue is that therapists are particularly skilled at introducing into therapeutic conversations extensions and perspectives that clients might appropriate into their own theories, thus elaborating these theories and enabling their eventual revision. While this general position seems reasonable enough, the question remains as to how such therapist-induced elaborations, even if developed collaboratively between therapist and client during the therapeutic conversation, become acceptable to clients. In short, what enables clients to accept and adopt theoretical extensions and elaborations that eventually might transform their theories about themselves, others, and their own circumstances? A possible answer to this important question is found in the work of Hazel Markus (1983; Markus & Nurius, 1986) on *possible selves.*

Consistent with the general template for human change adopted in this book, Markus (1983) believes that individuals extract theories of themselves from the events they experience in their lives. Self-theories develop around "those aspects of the self that become personally significant in the course of social interactions and they reflect domains of underlying salience, investment, or concern" (p. 548). These theories become progressively more elaborated and differentiated with increased personal experience, mediated through the memories individuals retain of significant events in their lives. (Markus actually uses the terms *self-concepts* and *self-schemas.* However, there is little in her articulation of her theory to indicate that my substitution of the term *self-theories* would be inappropriate.)

Of direct relevance to the issue of how clients might acquire elaborated, revised theories of self is Markus's conceptualization of self as a multifaceted, dynamic structure (theory) (cf. Markus & Nurius, 1986; Markus & Wurf, 1987). An individual's complete self-concept (or theory) actually is made up of various representations of self that are *potentially* available to the conscious awareness of that individual. The contents of a person's self-theory at any given moment (i.e., the *working* self-concept or *working* self-theory) are some subset of the contents in the complete self-concept. In addition to those self-representations (propositions, beliefs, images of oneself) readily at hand in the working self-theory are many other self-representations that are potentially available in the complete self-theory.

The self-representations potentially available to an individual's working self-theory vary in their structure and function. Some are well developed and fully elaborated, and might be considered to be central or core to an individual's complete self-theory. Others are more peripheral and less well elaborated. Some are positively valanced, while others carry negative affective, attitudinal associations. Thus, like Kelly's formulations of personal constructs, Markus's articulations of self-theories emphasize an integration of epistemic and motivational functions. Finally, and most important for the current purposes, *self-representations may or may not actually have been achieved.* Memories of significant life experiences inevitably enable guiding images for both achieved and potential (or possible) self-representations. Possible selves are theories of potential selves that are formed on the basis of imaginings built on past experiences, vicarious experiences, and information acquired about others and life in general.

For example, my self-perceived potential as a best-selling novelist clearly derives from my actual experiences in writing academic nonfiction (such as the current volume), my acquaintance with several writers of fiction, my knowledge of the biographies of certain prominent writers, and my own fantasies based on synthetic constructions of this information. I have not achieved my "novelist possible self," but it exists alongside (but currently on the periphery of) my actualized selves in my complete self-theory. Depending on my current circumstances, it may become a peripheral component of my working self-theory (as, for example, when I use my word processing system to compose texts like this one). My working self-theory is a "continually active, shifting array of accessible self knowledge . . . [that] consists of [my] core self-conceptions that are tied to the prevailing circumstances" (Markus & Wurf, 1987, p. 306).

According to Oyserman and Markus (1990), "the motivation to carry out all but the most routine and habitual actions depends on the creation of possible selves" (p. 113). Personal goals are more likely to be achieved if they can be associated with possibilities for the self in the future. Of course, the more similar future possible selves are to current, achieved selves, the more likely the attainment of the goals with which they are associated (assuming, of course, a general positive valence to the constituent self-representations).

In psychotherapy, the therapeutic conversation has the potential of assisting a client to elaborate, and subsequently to internalize, potential self-theories that are available from his or her past and vicarious experiences and general knowledge. A therapist might attempt to promote elaboration and internalization of possible self-theories whenever such theories may be associated appropriately with a client's therapeutic goals. Once internalized, these more elaborated, more fully articulated theories of possible selves gradually might force accommodation on existing theories of self. Eventually, such accommodations might lead to significant revisions to the client's working and complete self-theories, revisions that are supportive of desired changes in the client's modes of experiencing and behaving.

THERAPEUTICALLY INDUCED
PERSONAL THEORY REVISION

The theoretical work of scholars like Kelly (1955), Guidano and Liotti (1983), Harré (1984), Taylor (1989, 1991), and Markus (1983; Markus & Nurius, 1986) contributes to an understanding of personal change as the revision of personal theories. Individuals hold theories of themselves, others, and their own life circumstances that contain both epistemic and motivational properties. These theories support the perceptions, conceptualizations, and actions of those who hold them. Such personal theories are believed to arise from individuals' experiential recollections of their participation in past conversations and practical activities (as opposed to arising primarily from some set of genetically determined, biological structures or human capacities). Through such theorizing, an essentially nondualistic, holistic formulation of human agency and change is attained.

When set in the context of psychotherapy, this formulation of human change encourages a view of psychotherapy as a unique form of conversation that attempts to alter the personal theories of clients. These theories have been formed as a result of past experiences in other conversations, but somehow are dysfunctional with respect to the attainment of clients' goals in their current life contexts. By assisting clients to elaborate their theories of self, others, and life circumstances, therapists can help clients to revise these theories, first in the public therapeutic conversation, and then (through internalization of the therapeutic conversation) privately in their own understandings and beliefs. As seen in the previous chapter, the mediational role of clients' episodic memories, as vehicles for the internalization of relevant extratherapeutic and therapeutic conversations, is critical to the general processes of elaboration and revision of clients' personal theories through psychotherapeutic intervention. Possibilities for revising personal theories that are resident in clients' own experiences, but currently are not central elements in existing personal theories, may play an especially important epistemic and motivational role in psychotherapeutic change.

To illustrate the full process of the therapeutically induced elaboration and revision of personal theories, I present an actual therapeutic conversation taken from a sixth session of psychotherapy devoted to assisting a man in his thirties to understand and improve his intimate relationships with women. The psychotherapist is a middle-aged man who employs a combination of experiential, cognitive, and analytic therapeutic interventions. By this time in therapy, an initial elaboration of the client's current theory of his difficulties has been attempted. On the basis of this therapeutic work, it seems that the client believes he is extremely "open" in his relationships with the women he dates, as he believes he was with his now-estranged first wife. He thinks that his difficulties in forming satisfying, lasting relationships with these women results from their unwillingness to reciprocate his emotional and intellectual "openness." However, his inability to understand why such reciprocation is not forthcoming leaves him frustrated and angry.

In the fourth and fifth sessions of psychotherapy (each session lasting approximately 50 minutes, with sessions spaced approximately one week apart), the client illustrated the foregoing theory by describing a series of recent interactions with women, and past interactions with his former wife. At the therapist's urging, he attempted to articulate his *own* experiences and reactions to these interactions, as a supplement to the essentially third-person accounts he had been providing thus far, as support for his existing theory of his relationship difficulties. Only when asked to "reenter specific, recollected scenes" could the client begin to verbalize his own experiential reactions to them. These reactions consisted of mounting frustration and anger at his inability to extract, and at his partner's seeming inability to furnish, details of her own experiential reactions to him and to their activities together. The intensity of these emotions clearly surprised the client.

In the sixth session, the therapist and client began to explore possible contributions to the client's current manner of relating to women that might arise from his past and current experiences in his family of origin. In the following excerpt from this session, the therapist makes purposeful use of concrete, figurative language in an attempt to assist the client to probe his emotional experiences when interacting with his parents. Following the completion of the session, the client recalled part of this therapeutic conversation (C5 to C11) as especially memorable.

Client: My mother is a very, very caring person, and in that way I love my mother a lot. Very emotionally strong, although she thinks she's not. She can put up with a lot more than Dad can. He just pulls away, and denies any emotional component. [C1]
Therapist: He deflects it. [T1]

Client: Onto my sister a lot. Whoever the hell he can who's handy. He gets quite upset when you talk about his emotions. You're not supposed to have any. As a kid, he used to talk about being rational all the time. Rational was the best way. You can't give in to your emotions or weaknesses. I remember all that and now it's coming back. It's crap, all of it. [C2]

Therapist: As I sit here, I think of you as carrying a big emotional burden. [T2]

Client: Hmm. For whom? And why? [C3]

Therapist: I don't know. It's just an image I have of you carrying a lot of weight. Maybe some of his weight that he won't carry. [T4: In a postsession interview, the Therapist identified this comment as the start of what he considered to be an important section of the therapy session. At this point, he began to employ concrete, figurative language in a purposeful effort to facilitate the client's experiential elaboration of his "story."]

Client: Hmm. Like a sponge, taking all the deflections. I let it go right through me instead of bouncing back. And really, it's not my place, any of that. If that's true. [C5: The Client recalled this comment as the beginning of a memorable event in this therapy session.]

Therapist: Yes, if that's true. Turn inside, and focus on how it feels when you're at home. Your Dad starts doing his thing. Your Mom does her thing in response to him. And you're in the middle. How does that feel? [T5]

Client: It feels like I have a knot in my stomach. It feels unnatural. It doesn't feel like I can be myself in that setting. A stranger in a strange land with my own parents. Like I'm being something that I have to be. And playing a role that is necessary in that situation. [C6]

Therapist: That knot in your stomach. It gnaws? It weighs you down? [T6]

Client: It keeps me down. It holds me back. It prevents me from probably being who I am. Saying exactly what I feel. [C7]

Therapist: It's a restraining knot. [T7]

Client: Yeah. It's holding me back from, I don't know, possibly hurting somebody by being brutally frank about what I'm seeing, what I'm experiencing. [C8]

Therapist: You are restrained with your parents, and you're weighted down inside yourself. [T8]

Client: Hmm. It's almost like a control element for them. They can restrain me, hold me back. [C9]

Therapist: Whatever happens, perhaps you and they in combination,

holds you back. But, the end result is that you feel burdened.
(pause) The knot not only restrains, but it also gnaws. [T9]
Client: *Yeah. Yeah. I'm sure there is a lot of that. About my sister, and*
not being able to tell them about that—her being gay, even though
they suspect. And a lot of my Dad's emotional crap that gnaws at
me. My mother's incessant need to try and make up for 20 years of
my childhood that are dead now, that are gone and can't be made
up for. That gnaws at me. When will this end? She, we persevered
and got through her mental illness, the hellish times until I was—
what the hell was I? I guess I was 20 when she stopped having the
real severe problems. We went through it. It's done. I don't want to
have to relive it, and she constantly wants to relive this crap again.
It's not so bad now. It's been getting better, I have to agree, as time
goes on, but there's still a lot of crap. There's a lot of concealed
stuff that I don't think should be concealed. I tend to be probably a
little too honest sometimes, and people get hurt. And that's the one
thing I don't like about me is that I can be too honest sometimes.
And in this context, with you, I think that's what I'm being. And if
I went home and was as honest as I am with you, I would probably
"dissemble" the entire family. [C10: The client moves from obvious
anger to sadness (moist eyes) to brief, sarcastic laughter throughout
this talking turn.]
Therapist: *If you gave up all the psychological weight you carry for ev-*
erybody, all the secrets, it would destroy your family. Intolerable.
[T10]
Client: *Yeah. Yeah! [C11: This talking turn ends one of two therapeutic*
events recalled by the client as especially important in this sixth ses-
sion of therapy.]

The client's recollection of the foregoing therapeutic conversation
during the sixth session of psychotherapy subsequently mediated an important revision to his personal theory of his relationship difficulties. In
sessions seven and eight, the client and therapist elaborated the client's
theory of his relationship difficulties by linking his now-verbalized experiences in his family of origin to his experiences in intimate relationships
with women. In these jointly constructed, elaborating conversations, the
client was portrayed as an individual who was most comfortable when
he was in receipt of others' "secrets," and whose intimate, interpersonal
interactions were aimed at securing such knowledge from his partners.
What the client understood to be his "openness" in such situations was
an openness to the intimate expressions of others, rather than an openness to expressing his own emotions ("secrets"). This was especially true

with respect to any expression of what he referred to as "softer, less masculine" emotions like love, caring, and "needing," the expression of which he believed would leave him vulnerable to women who possessed knowledge of these "secrets." When his attempts to extract his partner's secrets were unsuccessful, he became worried that his own feelings of love and attraction might not be reciprocated. This worry inevitably led him to "cover up his own secrets" and to become upset and angry that his feelings for his partner might be too one-sided. Knowledge of this pattern of private experiencing and intimate interaction was new to the client and certainly never had been discussed openly in any of his past, intimate interactions with the women in his life.

Eventually, the client became sufficiently convinced of the possible veracity of the foregoing therapeutically elaborated theory of his relationship difficulties that he was able to take it outside of the therapeutic conversation (i.e., to internalize it through the mediation of his episodic recollection of the therapeutic conversations during which the theoretical elaboration had been achieved). At the therapist's urging, and in spite of his initial misgivings, he began to discuss his "softer" feelings with his current partner, in advance of requesting similar disclosures from her. Fortunately, in this instance his current partner, although somewhat "put off" by the client's previous attempts to "extract her secrets," really did seem to care deeply about the relationship and welcomed his expressions of love, caring, and vulnerability. Thus, toward the end of therapy, the client's episodic memories of previous therapeutic conversations containing elaborations of his personal theory of his relationships with women seemed to have enabled rather dramatic revisions to his private, individual theory of himself in intimate relationships. These revisions enabled him to engage in new forms of behaving and experiencing in relevant extratherapeutic contexts. Clearly, the client's actual and vicarious, past and current extratherapeutic experiences, together with his therapeutic experiences, had equipped him with sufficient material with which to construct a new (possible) theory of himself in intimate relationships with women.

The mediational role played by the client's episodic memories of past, extratherapeutic conversations and experiences (in both the therapeutic elaboration, and the extratherapeutic revision of, his theory of intimate relationships) is readily apparent in this case reconstruction. The therapist's use of expressive, figurative language (together with other therapeutic vehicles such as experiential support, encouragement, interpretation, and challenge) seemed to enhance the memorability and potential impact, for purposes of personal theory revision, of important parts of the therapeutic conversation.

Whether the revisions to their personal theories that clients experience as a consequence of participation in effective psychotherapy are expressed in terms of the *personal construct* language of George Kelly, the *self as theory* language of Rom Harré, the *ethical, agenic "I"* of Charles Taylor, or the *complete, working, and possible selves* language of Hazel Markus, such revisions may be seen as the primary goals of psychotherapy. They are the end products of the processes of conversational elaboration of personal experiences, and memory-assisted internalization of conversations and experiences, that have been the topics of this and previous chapters in this book.

EMPIRICAL EVIDENCE

Own Research

Support for several of the empirical claims contained in the foregoing account of personal theory revision in psychotherapy derives from three types of studies my colleagues and I have conducted in our ongoing program of research on psychotherapeutic change. Case study research (in which we have employed the methods of stimulated recall and free association/conceptual mapping described toward the end of chapter 2) has helped us to understand better the nature of changes to the therapy-relevant, personal theories of individual clients that take place during, and subsequent to, their participation in psychotherapeutic interventions. Both the case study described in chapter 2 (cf. Martin, 1987) and the case illustration employed in the immediately preceding section of this chapter are taken from work of this kind.

In conceptual maps produced by several clients over time in therapy, we have been able to detect gradual increments in the complexity, comprehensiveness, orderliness, and integration of clients' theories of themselves and their problems (Martin, 1987, 1992; Martin & Reaume, 1988). A feature of our conceptual mapping results that we believe to be particularly important is a general increase in the hierarchical organization of the personal theories of many clients as therapy proceeds. Such increased organization is a common feature in the knowledge structures of effective, expert problem solvers in a variety of areas of human activity (cf. Chi, Glaser, & Rees, 1982) and may reflect increased personal problem-solving expertise of clients as they advance through psychotherapy. Clients who have met with greater therapeutic success tend to display more obvious increments in the hierarchical organization of their therapy-relevant theories over the course of psychotherapy than do clients whose therapy is less successful (Martin, 1992).

Results obtained from client responses to our conceptual mapping task, when set against transcriptions and tape recordings of actual therapy sessions, indicate a clear relationship between salient conversational themes and content during therapeutic conversations and client's free associative, conceptual mapping responses. We consider such relationships as evidence of clients' internalization of important aspects of the therapeutic conversation into their own theories of themselves and their problems. For example, in the case discussed previously in this chapter, the client not only recalled the excerpted portion of his sixth session of psychotherapy as especially memorable, but also drew connecting lines between the free associates "own family," "secrets," "secret-holder," "[name of his current female partner]," "[his own name]," "frustration," and "hurt" on the conceptual map he produced following this session. These links had not been present in his responses to this task following any of the five previous sessions of psychotherapy.

When the foregoing results obtained in our case studies are combined with our general categorization of clients' recollections of important therapeutic events (into the general therapeutic tasks of *enhancing clients' personal awareness* and *revising personal theories*—see chapter 2 and Martin, 1992), the emergent empirical picture of clients' cognitive/experiential reactions to psychotherapy is quite consistent with the model of personal theory revision described in this chapter. Of course, given the inevitable alteration of rational and empirical phases that typifies any ongoing program of psychological research, some such correspondence probably is inevitable. However, the internal cohesion between our theoretical formulations of therapeutic change and our empirical data is not the only kind of support for our model of personal theory revision during psychotherapy. Independent research and theorizing by others also tend to support the essential thrust of our formulations. But, before turning to the work of others, I want to present the results of a recent study that supports a possible causal relationship between clients' memory-mediated internalization of therapeutic conversations and successful therapeutic outcome. While this study does not speak directly to personal theory revision per se, it lends considerable support to the idea that clients' episodic memories of therapeutic conversations are important mediators between therapeutic conversations and the benefits that clients perceive from their participation in these conversations.

Specific hypotheses in this study (Cummings, Hallberg, Martin, & Slemon, 1992) were that: (1) clients and therapists would display better *accuracy* of recall for therapeutic events from sessions they rated as more effective, and (2) there would be a greater *match* (similarity) between therapist and client recall of therapeutic events from sessions rated as more effective. The rationale for the former hypothesis was that the effectiveness of therapy sessions is mediated, at least in part, by accurate episodic memories for events in those sessions—the more active and accurate the encoding and recall (i.e., internalization) of therapeutic events and content by participants, the more effective and helpful the session. The rationale for the second hypothesis was that coincidence or overlap between clients' and therapists' episodic memories for session events indicates a strong empathic bond and working alliance between therapists and clients, the presence of which should be associated with perceptions of greater session effectiveness by the participants. In terms consistent with those employed in this chapter, such a match could be interpreted as indicative of collective elaboration of clients' personal theories by the therapist and client working together.

Data from 11 dyads of short-term psychotherapy (7 to 16 sessions each) were obtained. Accuracy and match of participants' episodic memories were measured by rating scales developed by the researchers and applied to data obtained from audiotapes and transcriptions of the therapy sessions and from asking therapists and clients to recall the most memorable events that occurred in therapy sessions in which they participated. Outcome measures were the Session Evaluation Questionnaire (Form 4, Stiles & Snow, 1984) and the Target Complaint Technique (Battle et al., 1965).

Results were that clients displayed greater accuracy of recall for important therapeutic events from sessions they rated as more effective on the Session Evaluation Questionnaire. There was also greater matching between therapists and clients in their recall of important events from these same sessions. In addition, a moderately high correlation (.48) between the "improvement in therapy" score (calculated across sessions for each dyad) from the Target Complaint Technique and client accuracy of recall was found that probably merits further consideration in research with more diverse therapy dyads.

These results can be interpreted as support for a potentially important role played by participants' episodic memories for therapy events in mediating between therapeutic conversations and therapeutic outcomes. Interpreted from the perspective of psychotherapeutic change as personal theory revision, these results are consistent with the general idea that the accuracy with which clients internalize important aspects of co-constructed, therapeutic elaborations of their personal theories enables them to derive benefit from their participation in therapeutic conversations. That the actual form of this benefit is in terms of personal theory revisions that enable more functional experiences and responses in relevant extratherapeutic contexts is beyond the scope of this study, but is supported by the case study research discussed earlier.

Other Research

I know of no other attempts to examine directly the products of clients' personal theory revision during and following psychotherapy through the use of methods such as the free association/conceptual mapping task that we have employed in our own research program. However, a good deal of empirical work is available in the general literature on psychological counseling and therapy that may be interpreted as consistent with the basic formulation of therapeutic change as memory-mediated personal theory revision.

Most obviously supportive of the theoretical perspective taken in this chapter are numerous detailed case studies of client change by Bonanno (1990), Edwards (1990), Guidano and Liotti (1985), Liotti (1986), and Rice and Saperia (1984), some of which I have drawn upon in previous parts of this book. All of these authors emphasize structural changes to clients' understandings of themselves, others, and life circumstances that result from their participation in psychotherapeutic interventions. Such interpretations are generally consistent, but not isomorphic, with my own characterizations of such phenomena.

Historically, less formal descriptions and interpretations of case studies that are generally consistent with my emphasis on clients' revisions of their personal theories, come from the work of major figures in psychotherapy such as Alfred Adler (1963), Eric Berne (1961), and Milton Erickson (cf. Rosen, 1982). Adler's teleological approach to therapy emphasized the investigation and reorientation of the *life-styles* of individual clients. Berne's approach centered around his conception of life *scripts,* with therapy viewed as a *rescripting* process. Erickson emphasized clients' *stories* (myths) that could be *"reframed* metaphorically" during psychotherapy. All these perspectives have been illustrated in numerous case studies presented by these psychotherapists, their students, and co-workers. All endorse the general notions that clients construct personalized systems of meaning through some general process of social-cultural internalization, and that psychotherapy works by somehow enabling clients to alter these personalized systems of meaning in ways that prove more functional with respect to the attainment of clients' goals.

Perhaps the largest body of contemporary empirical literature in psychotherapy, aside from the case study work cited above, that may be taken as supportive of therapeutic change cast as personal theory revision, has been stimulated by Aaron Beck's (1967, 1976) approach to understanding and treating depression. Beck believes that *depressive schemas* are negative views (informal theories) of the self, the world, and the future. These negative schemas operate in the experience of depressed individuals to bias negatively their cognitive/perceptual processing and behavioral selection in ways that continuously confirm the content of these schemas. Empirical research in this tradition has focused on analyzing the functions of depressive self-schemas, which are defined as hierarchically organized bodies of knowledge stored in clients' long-term memories.

A prototypic study of this sort was conducted by Derry and Kuiper (1981), who employed a self-referent, incidental recall procedure to study the relationship of self-schemas to depression. Three groups of subjects (depressed, nondepressed, and psychiatric controls) made three sets of judgments (self-referent, semantic, and structural) about a set of adjectives that featured either depressed or nondepressed content. Consistent with the view of self as a salient memory schema, all subjects recalled more adjectives in the self-referent condition. However, consistent with Beck's theory of depression, the depressed subjects recalled more depressed content adjectives. By measuring the speed with which subjects reacted to the content adjectives, Derry and Kuiper also found that depressives were more efficient than the other subjects in processing depressive information. Using variations to Derry and Kuiper's (1981) self-referent, incidental recall, and reaction time methods, a good deal of research (cf. Kuiper & Higgins, 1985) now exists that usually is interpreted as demonstrating how the negatively slanted, personal schemas (theories) of depressed clients bias their perceptions and interpretations of their life experiences as essentially sad, meaningless, and hopeless, and lead to behavioral patterns of withdrawal, excessive criticism, and general miserableness.

More recently, Toukmanian (1986, 1992), working in the general tradition of self-schema theory and research spawned by Beck's and others' application of information processing psychology to psychotherapy, has developed an instrument called the Levels of Client Perceptual Processing (LCPP) measure. She and her co-researchers have used this measure to study empirically changes to clients' actual in-therapy communications that might indicate changes to their self-structures and schemas. In conducting this work, Toukmanian makes two foundational assumptions.

The first assumption is that clients' internal representations (i.e. images, thoughts, impressions) of disturbing experiences are the *products* . . . of their experientially learned *ways* of constructing or perceiving "reality." Second, it is assumed that the manner in which clients talk about their difficulties is the most accessible index of how they organize and make sense of information regarding self and self in relation to significant others and situations in their environments. (Toukmanian, 1992, p. 89, italics in the original)

To date, Toukmanian and her co-researchers have succeeded in finding respectable empirical correlations between the in-session communications of clients and intermediate measures of therapeutic outcome. Those clients who evidence change, over the course of psychotherapy, to more differentiated and integrative (more elaborated) in-therapy discussions of themselves and their difficulties, as measured by the LCPP, tend to achieve more successful therapeutic resolutions of their concerns. While Toukmanian and her colleagues make no attempt to measure changes to clients' personal schematic structures (theories) directly, they interpret changes in the nature and manner of clients' contributions to actual therapeutic conversations as indicative of underlying schematic changes to their personalized systems of understanding and perceiving themselves, others, and their own circumstances.

THEORETICAL COHERENCE

If the personal theories of clients are equated (at least in a general way) with (1) the cognitive structures or *schemas* with which individuals organize information about themselves, others, and their own circumstances, and/or (2) the *stories* or narratives that individuals construct to make sense of themselves and their lives, a rather voluminous psychological literature may be seen as supportive of the general framework of theory revision presented in this chapter. Of course, the concept of personal theory connotes a more holistic, less mentalistic form of *personal meaning-making* than do terms like *cognitive schema*. Personal theories clearly are derived from one's experiences in social, cultural, and intimate contexts and include nonreducible affective, conative, and dispositional elements that are not always assumed in psychologists' conceptualizations of cognitive schemas. In these ways, personal theories are much more like personal stories. However, most conceptualizations of stories or narratives do not emphasize the hypothetical nature I envision for personal theories, particularly the ongoing, dynamic manner in which these theories are subjected to continual testing and revision in the context of new experiences in intimate, social, and cultural contexts. Nonetheless, the basic idea that individuals extract and organize understandings from their experiences that they then employ and "update" to enable them to perceive, anticipate, make sense of, and respond to their life experiences is common to all three formulations—theory, schema, and story. Thus, all three formulations are *constructivistic* in that they share the assumption that any understanding of human experience always is filtered through organizations of mind that derive from past experience, constrained by a small number of neurophysiological "givens."

Most reviewers of schema theories in psychology (cf. Brewer & Nakamura, 1984) trace the philosophical foundations of schema theory to the eighteenth-century works of Immanual Kant (1781/1969). While Kant maintained a form of Platonic essentialism in his assumption that divinely inspired, pure categories of mind transformed external-sensory experiences into meaningful representations, Karl Popper (1962, 1972; Popper & Eccles, 1977) provided a more contemporary foundation for constructivist theorizing about human understanding and action. Against naive forms of realism, Popper (1962) developed an epistemological position of hypothetical or critical realism (see chapter 1 for recent extensions of this position in the social and psychological sciences). Arguing against the views that observation is prior to theory, and that direct perception of the world is possible, Popper maintained that "nature as we know it, with its order and its laws, is . . . largely a product of the ordering activities of our mind . . . our cosmos bears the imprint of our own mind" (pp. 180–181).

Influential, initial empirical work in psychological schema theory was conducted by Bartlett (1932), who studied the influence of "old" knowledge on the perception and memory of new information. Bartlett defined schema as "an active organization of past reactions, or experiences, which must always be supposed to be operating in any well-adapted organic response" (p. 201). During the 1970s, influential theses by scholars like Minsky (1975), Neisser (1976), Rummelhart (1975), and Schank and Abelson (1977) provided the elaborated versions of schema theory that, in combination with the pioneering work of Kelly (1955), Beck (1967, 1976), and Frank (1972), have inspired numerous contemporary students of counseling psychology and psychotherapy (e.g., Mahoney, 1980, 1990; Pace, 1988; Turk & Salovey, 1985) to view psychotherapeutic change as the identification and alteration of dysfunctional schemas that underlie clients' problems.

Narrative or storied approaches to understanding human change processes in general, and therapeutic change processes in particular, also have much in common with the model of personal theory revision set forth in this chapter (e.g., recent work by Russell & Van den Broek, 1992). Narrative psychologists like Bruner (1986), Mair (1988), McAdams (1985), Polkinghorne (1988), and Sarbin (1986) have influenced several recent depictions of psychological counseling and therapy as "life-story elaboration, adjustment, or repair" (Howard, 1991, p. 194; also see this same source for a review of other work of this kind). These recent developments have highlighted the contemporary relevance of earlier construals of psychotherapy as an interpersonal, social process aimed at elaborating and revising the styles, scripts, and stories through which clients lead their lives (cf. Adler, 1963; Berne, 1961; Rosen, 1982).

Thus, the central idea of client therapeutic change as predicated on the elaboration and revision of clients' personal theories achieves rather extensive external coherence in cognitive schema and narrative psychologies applied to an understanding of psychotherapeutic change. I promote the notion of personal theory, over the related concepts of schema or story, because of the more holistic, less mentalistic connotations it holds. In emphasizing the *conversationally grounded, holistic* nature of the elaboration and revision of personal theories in psychotherapy, the current formulation of therapeutic change extends the work of George Kelly (1955), Guidano and Liotti (1983, 1985), and others who have conceptualized psychotherapeutic change in related terms.

It is, however, extremely important to emphasize the idea of *conversational grounding* of clients' personal theories. The current theory of therapeutic change does *not* assume that clients' theories of themselves, others, or their own circumstances can be altered as a direct consequence of therapeutic conversations alone. Because clients' existing theories, which support their current ways of being and behaving, have been appropriated from a lifetime of exposure to other conversations and associated practical activities, it is unrealistic to expect that theoretical alterations internalized from a relatively few therapeutic conversations will be realized easily in clients' extratherapeutic settings. Rather, it is the case that any revisions to clients' personal theories that have been initiated in therapeutic conversations (and associated therapeutic activities such as roleplays, behavioral rehearsals, homework assignments, and the like) somehow must survive the transfer from therapeutic to extratherapeutic conversations/contexts without reverting to the dysfunctional personal theories clients held prior to therapeutic intervention. How is this to happen if a client's extratherapeutic conversations and contexts do not support the holding of personal theories as therapeutically elaborated and revised?

It is all too easy to forget that all personal theories are situated in relevant social, interpersonal contexts, and that therapeutic change is not a facile, detached mentalistic exercise. The reason I have insisted on a contextually grounded approach to the acquisition, elaboration, and revision of personal theories is to avoid this mistake. Therapeutic change is not easy and cannot be accomplished outside of clients' ongoing extratherapeutic contexts and experiences. When Adler (1963) and Kelly (1955) advocated that clients be encouraged to behave *as if* they, and certain events in their lives, were different from what they previously had interpreted them to be, those theorists were encouraging more than a mentalistic reinterpretation or reframing. They were encouraging clients actively to transfer their newly revised theoretical perspectives to their real life experiences so that they could begin to accumulate direct experience in relevant extratherapeutic conversations and contexts, experience that might be appropriated as support for their revised personal theories. Without understanding what it means to possess personal theories by virtue of direct experience in real-world conversations and practical activities, it is all too easy for psychotherapists to underestimate the difficulties of promoting significant changes to the personal theories of clients in, and outside of, psychotherapy. An understanding of personal theory revision as a process that takes place at the interface of individuals' private experiences and their collective, social experiences allows psychotherapeutic conversations to be seen in their proper perspective — against the formidable background of other, past and ongoing conversations in the lives of clients who may be overwhelmed by difficult problems for which there are no easy solutions.

The holism assumed in my account of psychotherapeutic change also differentiates it from more mentalistic, schema-based accounts. As noted previously, Kelly (1955), Markus (1983), and others whose leads I have followed, do not separate cognitive and epistemic from motivational and affective processes and functions. In emphasizing the holistic representation of knowledge and values (gleaned from past experience) in individuals' personal theories, these approaches do not require separate formulations of cognitive, motivational, and emotional systems or subsystems involved in personal change. As Kruglanski (1989) states in summarizing his own, related theory of lay epistemics, such approaches make "the assumption that logic and motivation are inevitable parameters of any inference or judgment. This is in contrast to previous social cognitive views (like attribution or dissonance theories) that disjunctively stressed either the logical/informational or the motivational aspects of human reasoning" (p. 33). By following this tradition, I have attempted to provide an account of the revision of personal theories in psychotherapy that views personal change as a continuous, socially grounded process of theory testing and validation, in which public, social conversational experiences (inside and outside of psychotherapy) are basic to the personal understandings of individual clients.

Chapter 5

The Construction and Understanding of Psychotherapeutic Change

In our cognitive as well as in our active life we are creative. We add both to the subject and to the predicate parts of reality. (William James, 1907/1963, p. 167)

That humans, through their participation in intimate, social, and cultural conversations, develop theories about themselves and their circumstances is a basic premise underlying the explanation of psychotherapeutic change developed in this book. Memories of conversations, and the practical activities associated with them, are primary vehicles that mediate between these conversational experiences and participants' personal theories. Through the conversationally spawned, memory-mediated construction of personal theories, individuals are able to perceive, construe, and act in ways consistent with the achievement of personal goals. When emotional turmoil arises from frustrated goal achievement and/or disruptions and confusions in their life experiences, many people turn to psychological counseling and therapy as a means of support and assistance.

Psychotherapy is a unique form of conversation that attempts to alter clients' personal theories (theories that have been constructed on the basis of participation in other, previous and current, conversations) in ways that will support enhanced achievement of personal goals and resolution of, or coping with, personal concerns and problems. By working with clients to arrange therapeutic conversational experiences that will make certain pivotal understandings (as contained in particular therapeutic conversations and events) especially memorable to clients, psychotherapists attempt to assist clients to alter their personal theories. Over time, and with direct experiences in extratherapeutic settings, these memories, and the understandings they contain, can engender significant revisions to clients' personal theories. Such revisions can support new ways of being and acting in relevant extratherapeutic settings with respect to desired goal achievement and problem resolution/coping.

When considering the foregoing summary of the theory of therapeutic change advanced herein, it is essential to recall that my objective (see chapter 1) has been to set forth an empirically supported, theoretical explanation of how humans who experience effective forms of psychological therapy change as a consequence of their participation in the therapeutic enterprise. I have not attempted to specify what forms of therapeutic intervention are best, nor have I attempted to argue that psychotherapy is necessarily effective. Questions of *"what* works" have not been my focus. Rather, I have attempted to theorize about *how* psychotherapy, if effective, might work.

I have taken this approach because I believe that the kind of theory that I have attempted to advance has not been well developed in most extant research and theory concerning psychotherapy and therapeutic change. Perhaps it is simply pragmatic and sensible to attend to what works best and most effectively. Perhaps a concern about how something might work in the first place risks encouraging psychotherapists and students of psychotherapy to become "lost in thought," with little practical benefit to practitioners or clients in need of assistance. I have great sympathy with such arguments and great respect for providers of therapeutic intervention who attempt to "soldier on" in the face of widespread demand for their services. However, I ultimately am concerned less about being "lost in thought" than about being "missing in action."

There is an extremely diverse set of psychotherapeutic prescriptions currently available to practitioners and their clients. Numerous reviews of psychotherapy research have concluded that, in general, psychotherapy (in its most popular variations) does work, at least relative to its absence, and that particular forms of psychotherapeutic intervention may be especially effective for certain (although not all), specific client problems and difficulties (cf. Lambert, Shapiro, & Bergin, 1986; Smith & Glass, 1977; Smith, Glass, & Miller, 1980; Stiles, Shapiro, & Elliott, 1986). Questions of what forms of psychotherapy might work best for what types of clients with what kinds of problems and life circumstances are important and obviously will continue to fuel considerable empirical research.

Nonetheless, it remains true that our understanding of how psychotherapy achieves its effects is underdeveloped. As Mahrer (1988) has argued, the vast majority of past and contemporary approaches to psychotherapy have not been developed through theoretical advances of this sort. Rather, currently available psychotherapies have surprisingly weak theoretical underpinnings from one of two sources: (1) the personal theories and beliefs of leading psychotherapists, or (2) theories of human change that have been developed in other areas of psychology (e.g., psychologies of learning, development, and social interaction), mostly through experimentation in laboratory or analogue settings. Theoretical models of therapeutic intervention and change seldom have interacted with ongoing programs of research conducted in therapeutic settings per se (cf. Martin, 1991). There are signs that this state of affairs is beginning to change. Several contemporary scholars of psychotherapy have begun to recognize and articulate the importance of achieving a theory of psychotherapeutic change, grounded in empirical study of actual psychotherapeutic interventions, that attempts to enhance our understanding of how psychotherapy works (e.g., Rice & Greenberg, 1984; Strong & Claiborn, 1982; and others mentioned at various points throughout the previous chapters of this book). By forging what I believe is a unique synthesis and elaboration of relevant contributions from psychology and philosophy, with the results of my own and others' programmatic research on psychotherapeutic change, I hope to have contributed to this developing body of knowledge.

In this final chapter, I attempt a more formal statement of specific propositions in the theory of therapeutic change I have described and defended. I then consider how these propositions enable an enhanced understanding of therapeutic change, and go on to articulate the implications that they might hold for the practice of psychotherapy, the education of psychotherapists, and the study of psychotherapy.

THE CONSTRUCTION OF THERAPEUTIC CHANGE

The following 10 propositions, with accompanying elaborations, constitute a formal statement of the theory of therapeutic change with which I have been concerned in this volume.

1. Human experience occurs in the context of cultural, social, interpersonal, and personal conversations, and the practical activities associated with these conversations.
2. Human thought and forms of understanding, both conceptual and practical, are appropriated (internalized) from the conver-

sations and practical activities within which human experience unfolds.

3. Memories of experience in conversations and associated practical activities are primary vehicles for the appropriation of forms of thought and understanding.

4. Personal theories are belief systems based on appropriated forms of thought and understanding.

5. Such theories (about self, others, the world, and one's circumstances) support and enable perceptual, experiential, affective, motivational, and cognitive processes (e.g., values, reasons, dispositions, goals, and so forth) on which human actions are based.

6. When individuals' current theories and the actions they support do not permit the attainment of desired personal goals, acceptable resolutions to personal problems/concerns, or acceptable levels of personal coping, individuals suffer emotional upset and seek change.

7. Psychotherapy is a unique form of social conversation and interpersonal activity that attempts to help individuals to alter their personal theories so as to permit more effective goal attainment, problem resolution, or personal coping.

8. Psychotherapists work collaboratively with clients to elaborate their current theories by facilitating memory-mediated recall, interpretation, and analysis of past and current experiences and understandings in the therapeutic conversation. (Therapists' purposeful use of certain discourse such as imagery, metaphor, and other concrete, affectively laden language may facilitate such memory-mediated elaboration of clients' theories.)

9. Psychotherapists also work collaboratively with clients to help clients revise their theories once these have been elaborated. Such revision is achieved by clients' memory-mediated internalization of the therapeutic conversations and activities through which their theories have been elaborated, interpreted, and analyzed. (Memory-mediated revision to clients' personal theories is especially likely when content and understandings contained in the therapeutic conversation are perceived by clients as both *relevant* to, yet somehow *inconsistent* with, their existing personal theories. Both in-therapy behavioral practice and extra-therapeutic experience with new ways of behaving, enabled by therapeutically induced revisions to clients' theories, consolidate the revised theories and the altered actions and action tendencies associated with them.)

10. Ultimately, clients who have benefited from psychotherapeutic conversations and activities are potentially capable of contributing to the personal, interpersonal, social, and cultural contexts in which they exist in ways that alter these conversations and their experiences in them. (Having said this, it should be noted that the extent of such alteration is necessarily dependent on the strength of an individual's theories and actions relative to other factors that contribute to these same conversations and practices, with respect to their impact on the individual concerned.)

These 10 propositions describe the construction of therapeutic change as a special case, nested within the construction of human development and change in general. All psychotherapies, and participating therapists and clients, are embedded in the broader cultural, social, interpersonal, and personal contexts within which, and through which, human understanding and action arise. The constructive dynamics of psychotherapeutic change do not differ in kind from the more general constructive dynamics that enable all human psychological development and change. Psychotherapy is, however, unique in its socially and culturally sanctioned purpose of attempting explicitly to alter some of the more negative consequences of these more general dynamics within individual lives (see Frank, 1972).

UNDERSTANDING THERAPEUTIC CHANGE

The understanding of therapeutic change that emerges from the foregoing 10 propositions is *holistic, relatively nondualistic,* and *agenic,* yet includes important features that hold promise for a *critical realist* approach to therapeutic science (see chapter 1).

Holism

Experiences in conversations and the practical activities that accompany them, memories of those experiences, and personal theories extracted from such experiences and memories are holistic entities. They cannot be "broken down" into emotions, cognitions, motivations, actions, or various aspects of personality that exist apart from each other or from the totality of the experiences, memories, and theories in which they are embedded. Much contemporary psychology advocates a reductionistic analysis of human cognition, affect, motivation, and behavior that is built upon various mechanistic, computer metaphors for human functioning. The theory of therapeutic change presented here is nonreductionist and eschews subdivision of experiential, memorial, and theoretical units. Experience, memory, and theoretical understanding are complex, multifaceted phenomena that contain human emotions, motives, thoughts, and actions in indivisible, complex units that define these phenomena in real, psychological time and space. This holistic perspective is shared by many, although certainly not all, of the major sources (e.g., Vygotsky, Harré, Taylor, and Kelly) of the theoretical synthesis I have attempted to articulate. When I have employed sources (e.g., Tulving, Paivio, Markus) that are somewhat more reductionistic, I have incorporated them into the holistic framework I have adopted.

When a middle-aged client recalls a personally significant experience with her high school friends from which she has developed a central belief concerning the necessity of honesty in intimate relationships, it makes little sense to separate affective, cognitive, and behavioral aspects of the experiences, memories, and personal theories involved. It is enough to know that this experiential memory has influenced her understanding and current experiences of intimacy. If psychotherapists accept the inevitable mix of emotions, thoughts, and action tendencies associated with such phenomena, they are better able to comprehend their clients' experiences in real-life contexts. For psychotherapeutic purposes, such understanding is superior to that available from formal, reductionistic theories that psychologists have developed outside of these contexts. As was argued in chapter 1, the isolation of psychological phenomena from their relevant cultural, social, interpersonal, and personal contexts, whether for purposes of science or professional practice, alters these phenomena and prevents an understanding of them as they are manifest in the individual lives of clients.

Nondualism

The understanding of psychotherapeutic change promoted in this volume attempts to be relatively nondualistic as well as holistic. Following Vygotsky, Harré, Taylor, and others, I have attempted to avoid focusing exclusively on either private phenomena supposedly internal to individuals, or public phenomena supposedly external to individuals. Assuming only a small set of genetic, biological "primitives" (such as rudimentary sensory capabilities, a capacity for memory, a penchant for "making meaning," and a set of basic physiological needs), I have taken the position that psychological phenomena are derived from the cultural and social forms within which individuals live. This is not to say that I equate the personal/private with the social/public. Mine is not a form of correspondence theory. Rather, I believe that what is in mind and experience has its origins in the social-cultural practices and conversations within which experiences unfold and mind develops (see chapter 2). There is little of the psychological that does not originate in the social and the cultural, including the uniquely human capacities for reflection and agency.

When presenting episodic memory mediation as a primary vehicle for the internalization of social, public conversations and forms into personal, private theories, I have borrowed insights from more dualistic cognitive psychologies (e.g., the work of Tulving). However, I have attempted to incorporate what I have borrowed into the overall, relatively nondualistic perspective I have taken. Having said this, it also should be clear that the form of monism I have adopted still retains a distinctive place for psychological theorizing. Philosophically minded readers will note that in this sense my antidualism is more similar to that of Charles Taylor (1989) than to the eliminative materialism sometimes found in the work of Richard Rorty (1991b) or the strong antimentalism found in Wittgenstein (1953) and even in much of Harré's work (e.g., Harré, 1992). Like Vygotsky, I believe that the psychological originates in the social and cultural, but does not reduce to the social and cultural. I also believe in the inevitable uniqueness of individual human experience and in the potential of humans to "publish" psychological products (cf. Harré, 1984), occasionally leading to their adoption as social-cultural forms and practices. For these reasons, my nondualism is *relative,* situated between the more radical antimentalism of theorists like Wittgenstein (1953) and the more radical mentalism–individualism of much Western psychology.

Human Agency

The agenic character of human experience cannot be denied. Clients in psychotherapy, like all of us in our daily lives, are motivated by goals (perhaps Markus's images of possible selves) that guide intentional actions in the social, cultural, interpersonal, and personal contexts we inhabit. As Taylor (1989, 1991) has argued, there is nothing fundamentally incompatible with holding to a relatively nondualistic theory of human development and change that nonetheless admits the reality of human agency. As individuals gradually extract a theory of self from their interactions in their cultures, societies, and relationships, they are able to construct and elaborate increasingly rich and functional theories of themselves, others, and their contexts. From these theories, they are able to formulate intentions for actions that might achieve desired possibilities. Actions associated with personal goals and theories may enable individuals to contribute uniquely to their own life contexts, potentially influencing their own and others' experiences.

None of this happens outside of real social and psychological entities. By marrying social constitutionism with critical realism (see chapter 1), I have tried to articulate a holistic, relatively nondualistic framework for understanding therapeutic change. Human agency is enabled by clients' experiences, memories, and theories, and the ever-present potential for change resident in these dynamic phenomena (cf. Kruglanski, 1989). Thus, self-determination, within the constraints imposed by our social-cultural and interpersonal experiences (and the possibilities inherent in these experiences), is an ever-present fact of human existence. No adequate psychological account of human development and change, within or outside of psychotherapy, can afford to neglect this reality. Just like scientific theories, human reasons and personal theories inevitably are underdetermined by the data upon which they are based and that they attempt to explain. Human experience constrains, but does not entirely determine, our understandings, reasons, and purposes. The open-ended nature of our social and individual representations provides for the dynamic development and creation of personalized meanings and possibilities for action. As Greenwood (1989) states:

> Many human actions do appear to be self-determined by agents against a background of created personal meanings that embody their faith in and commitment to social, moral, religious, and scientific intuitions that extend by analogy, metaphor, and creative imagination way beyond the information given in the form of sensory inputs and cognitive rules. (p. 164)

Critical Realism

Critical realism, as expressed in chapter 1, holds that psychological phenomena are real entities that, although invisible, exert detectable causal force on social, cultural, and personal forms and structures. A client who has developed a personal theory replete with narratives of persecution and justifiable anger, may act, in seemingly similar contexts, in ways different from a client who has developed a personal theory of "bonhomie" and justifiable social confidence. Through appropriate probing of the psychological states and action tendencies of these two individuals, one might come to possess knowledge of their personal theories that would permit making claims concerning likely causal relationships between these respective psychological postures and the different behaviors and experiences of these two individuals in relevant social contexts. Any such claims will be based on an understanding of the psychological states of these individuals as situated and represented in particular social, cultural, interpersonal, and personal contexts. The admitted fact that such claims are difficult to construct and test in real-world contexts does not alter the reality of the entities assumed, or their testability, at least in principle (see chapter 1).

It is perhaps worth noting that the form of critical realism adopted herein is not completely incompatible with various systems of nonrelativistic interpretation developed outside of mainstream psychological science, including Gadamer's (cf. Widdershoven, 1992) historical hermeneutics and Habermas's (cf. Mendelson, 1979) critical hermeneutics. As Widdershoven (1992) has attempted to show, these positions share with critical realism an emphasis on culturally and historically "grown and tested ways of living" (p. 9) (i.e., nondualism and holism) and an emphasis on a process of critical reflection and debate characterized by free engagement (i.e., agency) as the essential means of human development.

The close relationship I have envisioned between psychotherapeutic change and a critical realist position with respect to psychological science is readily apparent in the following passage from Greenwood (1989):

> A realist science of action that accepts the possibility of human agency may have a quite different conception of the role of causal knowledge. Causal knowledge gleaned from experimental and other empirical inquiries may be employed and exploited to extend human powers and self-determination, and eliminate or alleviate human liabilities. This does not involve the prediction and control of others. Rather, it involves the transfer of control of action from stimulus conditions to human agents. It implies, for example, that the goal of moral education and much psychotherapy is the promotion and maintenance of human agency and self-control, and not the "engineering" of specific cognitions and emotions which themselves determine human action. (p. 174)

IMPLICATIONS FOR PSYCHOTHERAPY
PRACTICE, EDUCATION, AND RESEARCH

My purpose in this book has been to explicate and defend a theory of how psychotherapy works. While I have illustrated many of the primary propositions in my argument through actual therapeutic examples drawn from my own and others' research and clinical experience, I generally have avoided making specific prescriptions for psychotherapy practice, education, and research that might be implied by the theory I have articulated. This strategy has been purposeful, reflecting my conviction that psychotherapeutic science should be directed at generating and testing theories of therapeutic change. Such theories can help us understand how interactions between therapists and clients might assist clients to change their strategies and methods for resolving or coping with the problems they confront in extratherapeutic, real-life contexts. These theories, if supported by empirical research attesting to the feasibility of the change mechanisms specified, can provide *heuristic, conceptual* guidance to psychotherapy practitioners, educators, and researchers. However, because psychotherapeutic conversations and interactions are embedded in specific cultural, social, interpersonal, and personal contexts, the yield from any empirically supported theory of therapeutic change never can be *algorithmic* or *instrumental,* in the sense of offering tight prescriptions about exactly what sorts of therapeutic interventions will assist particular clients struggling to overcome their own unique problems.

The seemingly prevalent belief among many psychotherapy researchers and practitioners that therapeutic theory and research might provide such prescriptive, *instrumental* yield (see, for example, Garfield & Bergin, 1986), is, in my view, a mistake (see also Martin, 1990; Polkinghorne, 1991). Any theoretical/empirical program that studies psychotherapeutic change never will succeed in telling individual psychotherapists how best to work with different clients with different problems in different life contexts. There simply are too many possible sources of causal influence in any instance of attempted therapeutic change to permit such prescriptive specificity (see the latter part of chapter 1 for an explication of the problems of establishing and generalizing causal relationships in open systems). On the other hand, it is entirely possible for a well-supported theory of therapeutic change to be extremely useful to psychotherapy practitioners, educators, and researchers in a more heuristic, *conceptual* manner.

For example, the current theory might assist practitioners by encouraging them to probe the specific experiences, memories, personal theories, and action tendencies of individual clients. It also might encourage therapists to consider powerful memory-enhancing conversational methods with which to intervene during therapy sessions, so as to assist particular clients to elaborate and revise personal theories that seem likely to support more efficacious problem solving and extratherapeutic coping. Exactly what methods a therapist might best employ in any given circumstance must be left to the therapeutic acumen and artistry of individual psychotherapists. These cannot be specified in advance of the therapist's efforts to instantiate the theoretical template in the context of a particular case. Any attempt to do so inevitably will constitute a prescriptive (or psychological) fallacy.

I now want to indicate in more detail the sort of conceptual yield that I believe flows from the theory of therapeutic change I have presented. What follows should be understood as general counsel to psychotherapy practitioners, educators, and researchers about how they might understand their activities in practical, fruitful ways. What I have to say here should not be taken as a set of specific directions that might be followed to produce guaranteed therapeutic, educational, or scientific results. The implications I draw have the status of hopefully sensible understandings with practical implications. They are not step-by-step rules for constructing successful therapeutic, educational, or scientific programs in psychotherapy.

Psychotherapy Practice

I have conceived of psychotherapy as a corrective, enabling conversational experience between a properly qualified psychotherapist and a client or clients who require personal change so as to achieve desired goals or life states that they currently are unable to achieve. Essentially, therapeutic change involves the conversational, experiential elaboration and revision of clients' personal theories that are relevant to their problems and concerns. The therapeutic conversation and its associated activities promote such change by employing various sorts of communication vehicles and methods (e.g., metaphor and figurative language, dramatic argument, vivid roleplays and fantasies, affectively rich recollections, narrative structurings and restructurings, and so forth) that assist clients in constructing fuller, richer, more explicit and verbalizable personal theories than those they possess at the outset of the therapeutic endeavor. The social, conversational co-construction of these more elaborated theories is facilitated by clients' episodic memories of past and current experiences in relevant extratherapeutic conversations and activities. Once verbalized and experienced in the psychotherapeutic context, these revised theories are internalized by clients. Their episodic recollections of therapeutic conversations, experiences, and learnings enable them to experience and react to relevant extratherapeutic contexts in new and different ways — ways that are more effective and successful in achieving the ends they desire. Real-life experiences that serve to consolidate functional accommodation and change to clients' personal theories often are initiated in the therapeutic context itself through the vehicles of "homework" assignments, planned extratherapeutic exercises, preparatory fantasy dialogues, and roleplays. These and other methods anticipate and help to prepare clients for transferring their therapeutically elaborated theories and insights to their extratherapeutic life contexts in appropriate ways. Clients' episodic memories are critical mediators of both the theory elaboration and theory revision processes that lead to client change.

The literature on psychotherapy practice is replete with detailed descriptions of methods, strategies, and techniques that may be employed to stimulate elaborations and revisions to clients' theories. Any of these methods may prove effective in a particular therapeutic context, depending on the nature of the client's concerns, the nature of the therapeutic conversation, the therapist's expertise and personality, and a variety of other factors. In providing an overarching template for psychotherapy and psychotherapeutic change, I have not attempted, and do not intend to attempt, an anthology of change methods that are potentially available to therapists and clients. These are readily available elsewhere and may be selected for use by individual psychotherapists as they instantiate this or other conceptual models of therapeutic change in their actual work with individual clients or groups of clients. As I previously have indicated, I do not believe that it is possible to specify *a priori* what change methods or strategies are likely to be effective in individual instances of psychotherapy. Rather, I believe that such selection and employment should be left to the artistry of practicing psychotherapists.

My intention has been to provide a theoretical framework that may be adopted by practitioners to guide their conceptualization and understanding of their work. In practical terms, I view the theory of therapeutic change described herein as a heuristic model of *how,* in a general (perhaps even somewhat impressionistic) manner, psychotherapists might foster adaptive, functional client change. Determinations of exactly what methods to employ in individual cases of therapeutic interaction are the province of the professional psychotherapist, not the theoretician. My observations (both direct and indirect) of my own and others' therapeutic practice have helped me to develop and elaborate the theory of therapeutic change I have presented. In turn, this theory may be used by practitioners to understand and guide, in a general way, their work. It cannot tell them what to do in any sort of "cookbook" fashion.

There are, however, a few issues related to therapeutic practice that I want to address in more detail. These concern (1) the importance of the relationship between a therapist and a client, (2) much-discussed relationships between cognition, affect, and behavior in the fostering of personal change through psychotherapeutic intervention, and (3) cross-cultural considerations in the conduct of psychotherapy, especially with respect to clients who inhabit minority cultures.

   The therapeutic relationship. No effective psychotherapy can take place in the absence of a solid working relationship between therapist and client. In recent years, the emphasis on therapeutic relationship conditions that Carl Rogers and others (cf. Rogers, Gendlin, Kiesler, & Truax, 1967) attributed largely to personal characteristics of the therapist (e.g., empathy, regard, genuineness, and so forth) has been replaced by an emphasis on factors that contribute to a strong working alliance between the therapist and client as partners in the enterprise of therapeutic change (cf. Horvath & Greenberg, 1986; Marmar, Horowitz, Weiss, & Marziali, 1986). Bordin's (1975, 1976) conceptualization of the working alliance between therapist and client included three important factors: (1) a sense of agreement between therapist and client about the *goals* of psychotherapy, (2) a sense of agreement between therapist and client about the *tasks* of psychotherapy (i.e., that the specific activities engaged in therapy are reasonable, possible, and relevant to the goals), and (3) a sense of *bond* between therapist and client built on mutual trust, liking, understanding, and caring.

   The concept of relationship as a therapeutic, working alliance fits well with the template for therapeutic change I have developed herein. Therapeutic conversational partners, like other conversationalists discussing intimate, personal material, must be able to work cooperatively in order to elaborate relevant information. The kind of elaboration of a client's personal theories that is required as a prelude to revision of these theories cannot be accomplished unless the goals and tasks of the cooperative enterprise are acceptable and viable to both partners in the conversation. Further, both partners must care about these goals and tasks and must trust each other to expend real effort in advancing them. Through this shared work, if respectfully and thoughtfully engaged, emerges a genuine sense of personal liking, caring, and respect. In short, the affective aspects of the relationship between therapist and client (their personal relationship) cannot be separated from the nature of the activity in which they are engaged. When therapists and clients are able to establish viable, acceptable therapeutic goals, and to develop and execute tasks that advance these goals, they draw closer together. Their personal bond (relationship) cannot be understood outside of their conversational activities. It is not a function of their personalities as much as it is a function of their shared engagement.

   I believe that psychotherapists who understand the nature of psychotherapy (in this case, as a process of memory-mediated revision and elaboration of clients' personal theories) are more likely to contribute to the therapeutic conversation in ways that advance both the therapeutic relationship and psychotherapeutic change. By communicating such understanding to clients, therapists can help to ensure that the specific activities engaged are comprehensible. Within the context of a shared sense of what psychotherapy is all about, therapists and clients can work together effectively in an attempt to accomplish shared goals and tasks. The personal bond that is developed and strengthened by this shared activity may sustain increasingly difficult tasks of personal theory elaboration and revision as therapy progresses. A sensible, logical structuring and arrangement of therapeutic work from the beginning to the end of psychotherapy can enhance the likelihood that the working relationship between therapist and client will be as strong as is demanded by the difficulty of the tasks confronted. Ultimately, such relationships have considerable impact on the therapeutic elaboration and revision of clients' personal theories that may support more functional, effective forms of personal problem solving and coping.

Holistic versus reductionistic analyses of therapeutic change.

A second issue related to therapeutic practice that I want to address specifically concerns a tendency in many models of therapeutic change to reduce the change process to mechanisms thought to operate at separate, intrapersonal domains—that is, distinctive cognitive, affective, and behavioral systems. Not only are such conceptions of therapeutic change steeped in dualistic thinking, but they further assume that individuals can react to significant life events (such as participation in psychotherapeutic conversations) in partial, incomplete ways (e.g., cognitively and rationally, while somehow "bracketing" emotional reactions and behavioral tendencies).

All of the primary theoretical constructs employed in the theory of therapeutic change that I have presented are holistic, indivisible phenomena that encompass thoughts, feelings, and verbal and nonverbal activity (or the potential for such activity). During *conversations,* those engaged are simultaneously active at behavioral, cognitive, and affective levels. It is impossible to separate conversational utterances and accompanying actions into distinctive intrapersonal domains in any meaningful manner. People simply converse and experience the conversations in which they are involved, complete with their emotional reactions to them. Further, their motivations, beliefs, values, and preferences are shaped through their conversations and practical activities, and, in turn, find expression through their continued participation in these conversations and activities.

Memories of the sort I have discussed (i.e., memories for specific life experiences in conversations and associated practical activities) similarly cannot be divided into separate domain components. Such memories are replete with emotion, sensation, and active recollection, and are implicit conveyors of beliefs, values, and motives. They are autobiographical "snapshots" based on actual experiences that are similarly indivisible. Both experiences in conversations and episodic memories of these experiences are holistic entities that resist subdivision. While many approaches to psychotherapy that emphasize the role of individual memories are labeled appropriately as cognitive approaches (cf. Dryden & Golden, 1986; Mahoney & Freeman, 1985), it would be a mistake to construe the present theory in this way. Mine is not a cognitive approach any more than the work of Vygotsky, Kelly, Harré, Taylor, and others is cognitive. It is true that I have drawn on more cognitively oriented theories for partial support of my positions (e.g., the work of Paivio, 1971, 1986). However, my adaptation of the construct of episodic memory is made without any intention to carry forward "cognitivistic" assumptions about the divisibility of human experience, or the primacy of cognitive change over other forms of human change (cf. Lazarus, 1982). I treat episodic memory as an indivisible autobiographical, recollective vehicle that mediates between conversations and personal theoretical change in a genuinely holistic manner.

Finally, my use of the construct *personal theory* is similarly holistic and nonreductionistic. Such theories are no more than collections of meanings and understandings (both explicit and implicit) through which individuals perceive and construe experiences in their lives. They derive from practical experiences in conversations and related activities, and they enable individual actions in these contexts. Like conversations and episodic memories, personal theories include affective loadings, beliefs, values, preferences, motivations, and action tendencies. When I talk about the elaboration and revision of personal theories, I am talking about the expansion and refinement (for a client's purposes) of the corpus of informal meanings and understandings by means of which clients act in their therapeutic and extratherapeutic contexts. Such elaboration and revision may be stimulated in a variety of ways, including active experiences in and out of the therapeutic context. In my approach, personal theories are not divorced from action. There is no risk that clients will become "lost in thought" as they experience the kind of therapeutic change I have attempted to describe. Once again, personal theories derive from personal experiences (in the past, in therapy, and in current and future extratherapeutic contexts). They do not exist apart from the conversations and practical activities that spawn, sustain, and continually force revisions upon them.

Most North American and Western psychologists and psychotherapists have been steeped in the radically dualistic tradition of Western culture and thought. It is extremely difficult to break out of this tradition and the reductionistic psychology it fosters. I am not entirely sure that I have succeeded in doing so to the extent that I might have wished. However, my intent has been to provide a theory of psychotherapeutic change that is relatively unfettered by the problems and restrictions that radical forms of dualism and reductionism have placed on many psychological and philosophical analyses of psychotherapeutic change with which I am familiar.

The central implication for therapeutic practice of the holism I have attempted to preserve in my theoretical work may be stated rather simply. I believe that psychotherapists should spend less time being concerned with dualistic, reductionistic theories of therapeutic change, and more time experiencing and interacting with their clients as real people who simultaneously think, act, and feel in accordance with their historically collected cultural, social, interpersonal, and personal understandings. Therapeutic change as the elaboration and revision of personal theories can be entered into at many levels. Verbal analyses, planned recollections of past events, roleplays, fantasy dialogues, experiential exercises, homework assignments, and many other methods may assist different clients to elaborate and revise their networks of personal meanings and understandings and the action tendencies associated with them. It is up to individual psychotherapists to determine the specific methods and sequences of methods likely to stimulate such work in the different psychotherapeutic conversations in which they are involved. While I have offered some suggestions for the use of evocative, vivid, imagery-laden, emotionally rich language in the therapeutic conversation (see chapter 3), I do not wish to suggest that psychotherapy should be solely a verbal medium. The possibilities for the construction of active, in-therapy experiences that might assist clients to elaborate and revise their personal theories are almost without limit. Many different experiences, verbal and nonverbal, may prove appropriate in different therapeutic interactions.

The final selection of therapeutic interventions must be left to the informed artistry of individual psychotherapists familiar with the contexts and theories of individual clients. Recall (see chapter 3) that to be truly memorable, such interventions need to be perceived by clients both as *relevant* to their concerns and change projects and yet, simultaneously, as somehow *inconsistent* with their existing personal theories. The practical implication of this claim is that an effective psychotherapist must work continually at the interface of (1) the current epistemic state of a client's personal theories, and (2) those newly elaborated understandings embedded in the therapeutic conversation and experience. The essential epistemological task in psychotherapy is somehow to foster understandings that go beyond a client's existing theories, but that nonetheless can be perceived as relevant and potentially helpful, given these existing theories. Clearly, such informed, psychotherapeutic artistry inevitably must be highly contextualized and personalized. It cannot be overly prescribed by any general theory of psychotherapeutic change and practice.

   Cross-cultural considerations. The third, and final, issue with respect to therapeutic practice that I wish to address more specifically concerns the conduct of psychotherapy with individuals from differing cultural backgrounds. The central implication for therapeutic practice of the theory of therapeutic change developed herein is that psychotherapists must develop an understanding of clients' cultural backgrounds to an extent necessary to assist clients to elaborate and revise the personal theories they have extracted from the cultural and social conversations they have experienced in their lives. Without such understanding, it likely will prove difficult for therapists to work collaboratively with the clients they are attempting to help. This does not mean that psychotherapists must necessarily share the culturally embedded experiences of clients to the extent of being from the same cultural backgrounds. However, there is little doubt (other things being equal) that such shared cultural experience would increase greatly the probability that therapists would have the understanding necessary to stimulate clients to elaborate and revise their personal theories in aid of their attainment of personal goals.

   The difficulty with a radical form of cultural relativism in psychotherapeutic practice, which would demand that therapists work only with "same-culture" clients, is pragmatic. Even within the same culture, the experiences of individuals may be profoundly different, affected by wide variations in social class, educational opportunities, family and interpersonal styles, and philosophies of living. If psychotherapists were required to match their clients on all these variables in addition to cultural background, very little psychotherapy would be possible.

   A reasonable alternative is for therapists to recognize differences that exist between themselves (their past and current life contexts) and their clients, and to attempt to learn enough about clients' cultural backgrounds (both from listening carefully to clients' conversations and by learning from other sources) so that they can assist clients to change in ways that are sensitive to such differences. Attitudinally, psychotherapists must be willing to participate in therapeutic conversations and change efforts that might presuppose belief systems, values, and "rules of living" very different from those they have internalized from their own cultural experiences. Of course, ultimately therapists must be willing to recognize situations in which they cannot work effectively with culturally different individuals, either because they perceive such differences to be too vast or because they are not able to undertake the work and study necessary to better understand these differences. Given that the work of psychotherapy frequently requires therapists to "step outside" of their own experiential learnings to attempt to understand clients' personal theories, such decisions certainly are not unfamiliar to any practicing psychotherapist. In the final analysis, an effective psychotherapist must respect cultural differences and probe and guard against dysfunctional tendencies to "cultural chauvinism" that might be present in his or her own experiences and personal theories. A number of excellent reviews of literature capable of assisting psychotherapists in these regards have appeared in several journals of counseling and psychotherapy (e.g., Pedersen, 1991; Smith & Vasquez, 1985). Practical suggestions contained in the work of Allen Ivey (1988, 1991) may be especially helpful to many psychotherapists when working in cross-cultural contexts.

Before turning to implications for psychotherapy education, I want to attempt to clarify my suggestion for overcoming cultural relativism (at least in its more radical forms) at a more general level. In chapter 1, I argued that cultural and social practices, and their psychological products, were real entities capable of exerting causal force. The philosophical position of critical realism to which I adhere emphasizes the fact that such cultural and social practices are not especially ephemeral and that their effects can be long-lasting and resistant to change. Nonetheless, change can occur with the experience of different conversations and practices nested in different contexts. As Wittgenstein, Gadamer, Habermas, and others have pointed out (cf. Widdershoven, 1992), most cultures and people share a commitment to "ways of living" that have proven historically to be viable. Such forms of life generally are acquired by children with little in the way of critical reflection. Indeed, if these "bedrock" social conventions were challenged before they were experienced, they never would be acquired, and any future debating of them would be rendered impossible (cf. Wittgenstein, 1953). Nonetheless, as Habermas has argued (cf. Widdershoven, 1992), individuals (once past childhood) can come to reflect critically on their cultural heritage and experiences, to debate such matters, and to seek transcendent understandings that might conceivably bridge diverse cultural practices. As Charles Taylor (1992) recently has put it:

> What has to happen is what Gadamer has called a "fusion of horizons." We learn to move in a broader horizon, within which what we have formerly taken for granted as the background to valuation can be situated as one possibility alongside the different background of the formerly unfamiliar culture. The "fusion of horizons" operates through our developing new vocabularies of comparison, by means of which we can articulate these contrasts. So that if and when we ultimately find substantive support for our initial presumption, it is on the basis of an understanding of what constitutes worth that we couldn't possibly have had at the beginning. (p. 67)

It is this shared human capacity for critical reflection and debate, together with the generative nature of human discourse, that, in a more modest way, is precisely the basis for personal change and its promotion through psychotherapy.

Psychotherapy Education

To the extent that I have presented a viable theory of therapeutic change that is based on a memory-mediated, theory-revisionist template, the education of psychotherapists probably should focus less on prescriptive skill training and more on an understanding of therapeutic processes and change. What a therapist does to promote the elaboration and revision of a client's personal theories may vary greatly across different instances of psychotherapy, depending on factors such as the background experiences of both client and therapist, the client's current difficulties and life context, and so forth. Given these inevitable variations, tightly prescriptive therapist training that attempts to match specific forms of therapeutic intervention (including the exact skills and strategies to be used by therapists in individual cases of psychotherapy) to specific diagnoses of client problems and concerns in so-called *targeted* or *prescriptive* intervention models (e.g., Beutler & Clarkin, 1990) is not viable.

A sensible alternative to overly prescriptive diagnostic and skill training in psychotherapy education is a more general social science education at the graduate level, one that presumes a solid liberal arts and science background at the undergraduate level. Certainly, the acquisition of a broad repertoire of therapeutic skills and strategies has a place in the graduate education of psychotherapists. However, any such skill acquisition should be undertaken in the context of serious study of cultural, social, and psychological phenomena, through consideration of salient theories and problems, not only in psychology but also in sociology, anthropology, and philosophy (including the philosophy of social and psychological science). Interaction with social science disciplines other than psychology, and a detailed study of psychology itself (including social psychology, theoretical/philosophical psychology, experimental psychology, developmental psychology, and so forth), should be the norm. The sort of narrow-band, subdisciplinary professional training currently advocated by associations such as the American Psychological Association, Canadian Psychological Association, American Counseling Association, and others, should be replaced by a more scholarly program of studies in psychology and social science, under the control of scholars in our universities, albeit with necessary and desirable linkage to professionals and professional organizations so as to safeguard relevance and utility. Only in this way can psychotherapists acquire the kind of understanding of social science that I believe their practice requires.

More professional aspects of psychotherapy education (including the cultivation of a reflective, critical disposition toward one's professional practice and the "self-exploration" and personal development associated with effective therapeutic work) should not be neglected. However, much of this professional content and experiential learning is best addressed in pregraduation and postgraduation internships, under the tutelage of successful psychotherapists who themselves are well-versed in social psychological science and professional issues/requirements. More specialized practice that involves working with specific kinds of clients or within specific cultural contexts probably is best accomplished through similar internship placements. Indeed, it might be most sensible to arrange brief (but not too brief) apprenticeship placements in relevant practice settings for both novice and more experienced psychotherapists who want to begin working with clients, and in contexts, different from those represented in their own past experiences of psychotherapy.

Given the inevitable variation in human response to psychotherapy (as a consequence of cultural, social, interpersonal, and personal experience), I believe it makes sense to conceptualize the education of psychotherapists less as a kind of sophisticated professional training and more as a kind of immersion in relevant social science followed by appropriate apprenticeship in psychotherapy practice. However, it also is important to focus education in relevant social sciences on important questions concerning psychotherapeutic change and its promotion. Throughout the social science graduate education of psychotherapists, ethical, legal, professional, philosophical, and practical issues in psychotherapy should be considered and analyzed. In short, what I have in mind with respect to the graduate education of psychotherapists is a thoroughgoing grounding in relevant social science targeted at psychotherapeutic phenomena (although not exclusively), followed by apprenticeship experiences under the direction of thoughtful, reflective practicing psychotherapists.

Psychotherapy Research

In chapter 1, I described the critical realist framework from which I construe the theoretical and empirical approach to therapeutic change I have attempted to advance in this book. Perhaps the most important aspect of this framework is the explicit recognition that the subject matter of psychological, therapeutic science (i.e., human actions and psychological states) cannot be replicated in detached laboratory or analogue contexts. Because therapeutic phenomena cannot be studied outside of the actual therapeutic contexts in which they exist (for to do so would be to alter them), it is extremely difficult to test causal theories of therapeutic change, such as the one I have advanced. Too many factors, other than those most salient in specific theoretical formulations, can affect the course of therapeutic change. If the goal of psychotherapy research is to determine exactly what sorts of therapeutic interventions will work with what sorts of clients with what kinds of problems, such prescriptive yield never will be forthcoming from research on psychotherapy and psychotherapeutic change.

Consequently, I have consistently and purposefully promoted a theory that attempts to provide an empirically supported explanation of *how* psychotherapy might work. I think that this is a legitimate and obtainable goal for psychotherapy research. However, the yield from such work is not instrumental, but conceptual. The understanding that comes from the sort of theory-driven empirical research I have described in support of my theory cannot tell psychotherapists what to do at any given moment in therapy. Rather, it can act as a general conceptualization of therapeutic change and its promotion that therapists might instantiate and use as a framework for rational decision making in the context of their therapeutic efforts.

Thus, I believe that psychotherapy research can provide empirical support for theories of therapeutic change that provide viable causal explanations of how psychotherapy might work. To the extent that such theories are useful to practitioners in making sense of their therapeutic activities and in assisting them to provide more effective interventions to their clients, they can have considerable pragmatic utility. This is not to say that such an approach to psychotherapy research ever can determine precisely the complete set of causes for any individual instance of psychotherapeutic change. Instead, the more modest and sustainable claim of such a research program is that it might provide a form of progressive understanding of psychotherapy and possible generative mechanisms of psychotherapeutic change for both social psychological scientists and practitioners.

Obviously, I believe that research on psychotherapy should be conducted in ways that are theory-driven, are properly contextualized, and consider both the actions and experiences of clients and therapists. In this book I have illustrated my theory of psychotherapeutic change and some of its empirical support through the presentation of dialogue taken from actual psychotherapy sessions. I believe that the theory-driven intensive analysis of therapeutic discourse and participants' recollection of psychotherapeutic experiences is perhaps the best way in which to continue empirical testing of the theoretical propositions stated earlier in this chapter. Such discourse analyses may be combined with case designs similar to that used by Martin, Cummings, and Hallberg (1992). In such designs, therapist-experimenters would attempt purposefully to create psychotherapeutic dialogue and activities that they believe, based on their ongoing tracking of clients' understandings and experiences, clients will perceive as both relevant to yet inconsistent with therapeutically important aspects of their personal theories. Intensive case studies of this kind might employ a variety of recently developed methods of discourse analysis (e.g., Gee, Michaels, & O'Connor, 1992; Much, 1992), some of which (e.g., Jacob, 1992; Wertsch, 1991) have been developed from an explicitly neo-Vygotskian perspective. In keeping with the theory-testing warrant of *semipredictive utility* (see chapter 1), content and material from discourse episodes during which therapists engage in purposeful attempts at enhancing the memorability of clients' therapeutic experiences might be predicted to be represented in clients' perceptions and recollections of psychotherapy sessions, and subsequently in clients' altered personal theories relevant to their problems and concerns. A variety of stimulated recall and interview methods (see chapters 2, 3, and 4) might be employed to generate data relevant to interpreting such perceptions, recollections, and personal theories. Of particular interest would be longitudinal case studies in which such client variables are traced as they evolve over several years following the psychotherapeutic experiences of individual clients. For such work, I previously have suggested (Martin, 1992) methods such as structured journal entries and random follow-up probes administered over the telephone.

Because I previously have discussed such matters at some length (Martin, 1989, 1991, 1992), I will limit myself here to the foregoing summary of the kind of research I have in mind. However, in concluding this section, I want again to stress the importance of adopting a purpose for such research that differs from the more prescriptive purposes most frequently discussed in various extant proposals for the conduct of psychotherapy research. By advocating and demonstrating a focus on how psychotherapy might conceivably work, I have attempted to promote a goal for research on psychotherapy that is at once more modest and, hopefully, more attainable.

A FINAL WORD

At the outset of this final chapter, I quoted from William James to the effect that we (psychotherapists, psychotherapy educators, and psychotherapy researchers) contribute to reality (in this case, the social psychological reality of psychotherapy) both by our participation in it and our study of it. Psychotherapy is our creation, grounded in the historical and contemporary renderings that we give it by virtue of our cultural, social, and personal notions of psychological health and healing. As I have stated so frequently in this volume, psychotherapy is a conversation that attempts to alter our personal theories about ourselves and our lives. These are theories that we have extracted from our lifelong participation in our families, our friendships, our societies, and our cultures, but that currently do not serve us well in terms of reaching our goals, resolving our problems, or coping with our present life situations. Contemporary Western psychotherapy is simply a "professionalized" version of our quest to extract more meaningful understandings from our interactions with the world (physical and social) and others, especially with respect to ascertaining our own place in these interactions. I have focused attention on what I believe are important features and roles of psychotherapeutic conversations and memories with respect to the elaboration and creation of more viable, meaningful, and functional personal theories. In so doing, I hope to have contributed in some small measure to our ongoing attempts to understand psychotherapy as a uniquely human enterprise by which we attempt to help ourselves to live more useful, productive, and satisfying lives.

REFERENCES

Adler, A. (1963). *The practice and theory of individual psychology.* Paterson, NJ: Littlefield, Adams.

Anderson, J. R. (1983). *The architecture of cognition.* Cambridge, MA: Harvard University Press.

Angus, L. E., & Rennie, D. L. (1988). Therapist participation in metaphor generation: Collaborative and noncollaborative style. *Psychotherapy, 25,* 552–560.

Angus, L. E., & Rennie, D. L. (1989). Envisioning the representational world: The client's experience of metaphoric expression in psychotherapy. *Psychotherapy, 26,* 372–379.

Ashcraft, M. H. (1989). *Human memory and cognition.* Glenview, IL: Scott, Foresman.

Bakhtin, M. M. (1986). *Speech genres and other late essays* (V. W. McGee, Trans.). Austin: University of Texas Press.

Bartlett, F. C. (1932). *Remembering: A study in experimental and social psychology.* Cambridge, MA: Harvard University Press.

Battle, C. C., Imber, S. D., Hoehn-Saric, R., Stone, A. R., Nash, E. R., & Frank, J. D. (1965). Target complaints as criteria of improvement. *American Journal of Psychotherapy, 20,* 184–192.

Beck, A. T. (1967). *Depression: Clinical, experimental and theoretical aspects.* New York: Hoeber.

Beck, A. T. (1976). *Cognitive therapy and the emotional disorders.* New York: International Universities Press.

Berne, E. (1961). *Transactional analysis in psychotherapy.* New York: Grove.

Beutler, L. E., & Clarkin, J. E. (1990). *Systematic treatment selection: Toward targeted therapeutic interventions.* New York: Brunner/Mazel.

Bhaskar, R. (1989). *Reclaiming reality.* London: Verso.

Bonanno, G. A. (1990). Remembering and psychotherapy. *Psychotherapy, 27,* 175–186.

Bordin, E. S. (1975, June). *The generalizability of the psychoanalytic concept of working alliance.* Paper presented at the annual meeting of the Society for Psychotherapy Research, Boston.

Bordin, E. S. (1976, September). *The working alliance: Basis for a general theory of psychotherapy*. Paper presented at a symposium of the American Psychological Association, Washington, DC.

Bowlby, J. (1985). The role of childhood experience in cognitive disturbance. In M. J. Mahoney & A. Freeman (Eds.), *Cognition and psychotherapy* (pp. 181–200). New York: Plenum.

Brewer, W. F., & Nakamura, G. V. (1984). The nature and function of schemas. In R. S. Wyer, Jr., & T. K. Scrull (Eds.), *Handbook of social cognition* (Vol. 1, pp. 119–160). Hillsdale, NJ: Erlbaum.

Bruner, J. S. (1986). *Actual minds, possible worlds*. Cambridge, MA: Harvard University Press.

Bruner, J. S. (1990). *Acts of meaning*. Cambridge, MA: Harvard University Press.

Bucci, W. (1985). Dual coding: A cognitive model for psychoanalytic research. *Journal of the American Psychoanalytic Association, 33,* 571–607.

Chalmers, A. (1990). *Science and its fabrication*. Minneapolis: University of Minnesota Press.

Chi, M., Glaser, R., & Rees, E. (1982). Expertise in problem solving. In R. Sternberg (Ed.), *Advances in the psychology of intelligence* (Vol. 1, pp. 7–75). Hillsdale, NJ: Erlbaum.

Claiborn, C. D. (1988, August). Contributions of interactional theory to counseling theory. In J. W. Lichtenberg (Chair), *Contributions of interpersonal theory to counseling psychology*. Symposium conducted at the meeting of the American Psychological Association, Atlanta.

Claiborn, C. D., & Lichtenberg, J. W. (1989). Interactional counseling. *The Counseling Psychologist, 17,* 355–453.

Connerton, P. (1989). *How societies remember*. New York: Cambridge University Press.

Craik, F. I. M., & Tulving, E. (1975). Depth of processing and the retention of words in episodic memory. *Journal of Experimental Psychology, 104,* 268–294.

Cummings, A. L., Hallberg, E. T., Martin, J., & Slemon, A. G. (1992). Participants' memories for therapeutic events and ratings of session effectiveness. *Journal of Cognitive Psychotherapy, 6,* 113–124.

Cummings, A. L., Martin, J., Hallberg, E. T., & Slemon, A. G. (1992). Memory for therapeutic events, session effectiveness, and working alliance in short-term counseling. *Journal of Counseling Psychology, 39,* 306–312.

Danziger, K. (1990). *Constructing the subject: Historical origins of psychological research*. Cambridge: Cambridge University Press.

Davisson, A. (1978). George Kelly and the American mind (or why has he been obscure for so long in the U.S.A. and whence the new interest?). In F. Fransella (Ed.), *Personal construct psychology 1977* (pp. 25–33). New York: Academic.

Derry, P. A., & Kuiper, N. A. (1981). Schematic processing and self-reference in clinical depressives. *Journal of Abnormal Psychology, 90,* 286–297.

Dretske, F. (1982). The informational character of representations. *Behavioral and Brain Sciences, 5,* 376-377.

Dryden, W., & Golden, W. (Eds.). (1986). *Cognitive-behavioural approaches to psychotherapy.* London: Harper & Row.

Edwards, D. J. A. (1990). Cognitive therapy and the restructuring of early memories through guided imagery. *Journal of Cognitive Psychotherapy: An International Quarterly, 4,* 33-50.

Ellenberg, H. (1970). *The discovery of the unconscious.* New York: Basic.

Ellis, A. (1962). *Reason and emotion in psychotherapy.* Secaucus, NJ: Lyle Stuart.

Frank, J. D. (1972). *Persuasion and healing.* Baltimore, MD: Johns Hopkins University Press.

Frank, J. D. (1974). Psychotherapy: The restoration of morale. *American Journal of Psychotherapy, 131,* 271-274.

Freud, S. (1955). *The interpretation of dreams* (Ed. and Trans. by J. Strachey). New York: Basic Books. (Original work published 1900)

Freud, S. (1966). Introductory lectures on psychoanalysis. In J. Strachey (Ed. and Trans.), *The standard edition of the complete psychological works of Sigmund Freud* (Vol. 15, pp. 15-239; Vol. 16, pp. 243-463). London: Hogarth. (Original work published 1917)

Freud, S. (1966). From the history of an infantile neurosis. In J. Strachey (Ed. and Trans.), *The standard edition of the complete psychological works of Sigmund Freud* (Vol. 17, pp. 7-122). London: Hogarth. (Original work published 1918)

Freud, S. (1966). Remembering, repeating and working through. In J. Strachey (Ed. and Trans.), *The standard edition of the complete psychological works of Sigmund Freud* (Vol. 12, pp. 145-156). London: Hogarth. (Original work published 1914)

Friedlander, M. L. (in press). On the process of studying the process of change in family therapy. In L. T. Hoshmand & J. Martin, *Method choice and inquiry process: Lessons from programmatic research on psychotherapy practice.* New York: Teachers College Press.

Friedlander, M. L., Thibodeau, J. R., Nichols, M. P., Tucker, C., & Snyder, J. (1985). Introducing semantic cohesion analysis: A study of small group talk. *Small Group Behavior, 16,* 285-302.

Garfield, S. L., & Bergin, A. E. (Eds.). (1986). *Handbook of psychotherapy and behavioral change* (3rd ed.). New York: Wiley & Sons.

Gee, J. P., Michaels, S., & O'Connor, M. C. (1992). Discourse analysis. In M. D. LeCompte, W. L. Millroy, & J. Preissle (Eds.), *The handbook of qualitative research in education* (pp. 227-292). San Diego, CA: Academic Press.

Gergen, K. J., & Gergen, M. M. (1988). Narrative and the self as relationship. *Advances in Experimental Social Psychology, 21,* 17-56.

Glisky, E., Schacter, D. L., & Tulving, E. (1984, August). *Vocabulary learning in amnesic patients: Method of vanishing cues.* Paper presented at the meeting of the American Psychological Association, Toronto.

Gonçalves, O. F., & Craine, M. H. (1990). The use of metaphors in cognitive therapy. *Journal of Cognitive Psychotherapy: An International Quarterly, 4,* 135–150.

Greenberg, L. S. (1984). A task analysis of interpersonal conflict resolution. In L. N. Rice & L. S. Greenberg (Eds.), *Patterns of change: Intensive analysis of psychotherapy process* (pp. 67–123). New York: Guilford.

Greenberg, L. S., & Pinsof, W. M. (Eds.). (1986). *The psychotherapeutic process: A research handbook.* New York: Guilford.

Greenwood, J. D. (1989). *Explanation and experiment in social psychological science: Realism and the social constitution of action.* New York: Springer-Verlag.

Greenwood, J. D. (1991a). *Relations and representations: An introduction to the philosophy of social psychological science.* New York: Routledge.

Greenwood, J. D. (1991b). Reasons to believe. In J. D. Greenwood (Ed.), *The future of folk psychology: Intentionality and cognitive science* (pp. 70–92). New York: Cambridge University Press.

Guidano, V. F., & Liotti, G. (1983). *Cognitive processes and emotional disorders.* New York: Guilford.

Guidano, V. F., & Liotti, G. (1985). A constructivistic foundation for cognitive therapy. In M. J. Mahoney & A. Freeman (Eds.), *Cognition and psychotherapy* (pp. 101–142). New York: Plenum.

Harré, R. (1984). *Personal being: A theory for individual psychology.* Cambridge, MA: Harvard University Press.

Harré, R. (1992). Introduction: The second cognitive revolution. *American Behavioral Scientist, 36,* 5–7.

Heesacker, M. (1986). Counseling pretreatment and the elaboration likelihood model of attitude change. *Journal of Counseling Psychology, 33,* 107–114.

Heidegger, M. (1962). *Being and time* (J. Macquarrie & E. Robinson, Trans.). New York: Harper & Row. (Original work published 1927)

Heppner, P. P., & Claiborn, C. D. (1989). Social influence research in counseling: A review and critique. *Journal of Counseling Psychology, 36,* 365–387.

Hiley, D. R., Bohman, J. F., & Shusterman, R. (Eds.). (1991). *The interpretive turn: Philosophy, science, culture.* Ithaca, NY: Cornell University Press.

Horvath, A. O., & Greenberg, L. S. (1986). The development of the working alliance inventory. In L. S. Greenberg & W. M. Pinsof (Eds.), *The psychotherapeutic process: A research handbook* (pp. 529–556). New York: Guilford.

Howard, G. S. (1991). Culture tales: A narrative approach to thinking, cross-cultural psychology, and psychotherapy. *American Psychologist, 46,* 187–197.

Howard, G. S., & Conway, C. G. (1986). Can there be an empirical science of volitional action? *American Psychologist, 41,* 1241–1251.

Ingram, R. E. (Ed.). (1986). *Information processing approaches to clinical psychology.* New York: Academic.

Ivey, A. E. (1988). *Intentional interviewing and counseling: Facilitating client development.* Pacific Grove, CA: Brooks/Cole.

Ivey, A. E. (1991). *Developmental strategies for helpers: Individual, family, and network interventions.* Pacific Grove, CA: Brooks/Cole.

Jackson, D. D. (1961). Interactional psychotherapy. In M. I. Stein (Ed.), *Contemporary psychotherapies* (pp. 256–271). New York: Glencoe.

Jacob, E. (1992). Culture, context, and cognition. In M. D. LeCompte, W. L. Millroy, & J. Preissle (Eds.), *The handbook of qualitative research in education* (pp. 293–336). San Diego, CA: Academic Press.

James, W. (1963). *Pragmatism and four essays from the meaning of truth.* Cleveland, OH: Meridian. (Original work published 1907)

Jankowicz, A. D. (1987). Whatever became of George Kelly? Applications and implications. *American Psychologist, 42,* 481–487.

Kant, I. (1969). *Critique of pure reason.* London: Dent. (Original work published 1781)

Kelly, G. (1955). *A theory of personality: The psychology of personal constructs.* New York: Norton.

Kiesler, D. J. (1982). Interpersonal theory for personality and psychotherapy. In J. C. Anchin & D. J. Kiesler (Eds.), *Handbook of interpersonal psychotherapy* (pp. 3–24). New York: Pergamon.

Klein, M. H., Mathieu-Coughlan, P., & Kiesler, D. J. (1986). The experiencing scales. In L. S. Greenberg & W. M. Pinsof (Eds.), *The psychotherapeutic process: A research handbook* (pp. 21–72). New York: Guilford.

Kosslyn, S. M. (1980). *Image and mind.* Cambridge, MA: Harvard University Press.

Kozulin, A. (1986). Vygotsky in context. In L. Vygotsky, *Thought and language* (pp. xi–lvi). Cambridge, MA: MIT Press.

Kuiper, N. A., & Higgins, E. T. (1985). Social cognition and depression: A general integrative perspective. *Social Cognition, 3,* 1–15.

Kruglanski, A. W. (1989). *Lay epistemics and human knowledge: Cognitive and motivational bases.* New York: Plenum.

Lakatos, I. (1970). Falsification and the methodology of scientific research programs. In I. Lakatos & A. Musgrave (Eds.), *Criticism and the growth of knowledge* (pp. 91–196). Cambridge: Cambridge University Press.

Lakatos, I. (1978). *The methodology of scientific research programs.* Cambridge: Cambridge University Press.

Lambert, M. J., Shapiro, D. A., & Bergin, A. E. (1986). The effectiveness of psychotherapy. In S. L. Garfield & A. E. Bergin (Eds.), *Handbook of psychotherapy and behavior change* (3rd ed.; pp. 213–256). New York: Wiley.

Lazarus, R. S. (1982). Thoughts on the relations between emotion and cognition. *American Psychologist, 37,* 1019–1024.

Liotti, G. (1986). Structural cognitive therapy. In W. Dryden & W. Golden (Eds.), *Cognitive-behavioural approaches to psychotherapy* (pp. 91–128). London: Harper & Row.

Loftus, E. F. (1993). The reality of repressed memories. *American Psychologist, 48,* 518–537.

Loftus, G. R., & Mackworth, N. H. (1978). Cognitive determinants of fixation location during picture viewing. *Journal of Experimental Psychology: Human Perception and Performance, 4,* 565–572.

Mahoney, M. J. (1980). Psychotherapy and the structure of personal revolutions. In M. J. Mahoney (Ed.), *Psychotherapy process* (pp. 157–180). New York: Plenum.

Mahoney, M. J. (1990). *Human change processes.* New York: Basic Books.

Mahoney, M. J., & Freeman, A. (Eds.). (1985). *Cognition and psychotherapy.* New York: Plenum.

Mahrer, A. R. (1988). Discovery-oriented psychotherapy research: Rationale, aims, and methods. *American Psychologist, 43,* 694–702.

Mahrer, A. R., & Nadler, W. P. (1986). Good moments in psychotherapy: A preliminary review, a list, and some promising research avenues. *Journal of Consulting and Clinical Psychology, 54,* 10–15.

Mair, M. (1988). Psychology as storytelling. *International Journal of Personal Construct Psychology, 1,* 125–138.

Mandler, G. (1984). *Mind and body: Psychology of emotion and stress.* New York: Norton.

Manicas, P. T., & Secord, P. F. (1983). Implications for psychology of the new philosophy of science. *American Psychologist, 38,* 399–413.

Markus, H. (1983). Self-knowledge: An expanded view. *Journal of Personality, 51,* 543–565.

Markus, H., & Nurius, P. S. (1986). Possible selves. *American Psychologist, 41,* 954–969.

Markus, H., & Wurf, E. (1987). The dynamics of self-concept: A social psychological perspective. *Annual Review of Psychology, 38,* 296–337.

Marmar, C. R., Horowitz, M. J., Weiss, D. S., & Marziali, E. (1986). The development of the therapeutic alliance rating system. In L. S. Greenberg & W. M. Pinsof (Eds.), *The psychotherapeutic process: A research handbook* (pp. 367–390). New York: Guilford.

Martin, J. (1987). *Cognitive-instructional counseling.* London, ON: Althouse Press.

Martin, J. (1989). A rationale and proposal for cognitive-mediational research on counseling and psychotherapy. *The Counseling Psychologist, 17,* 111–135.

Martin, J. (1990). Confusions in "Psychological Skills Training." *Journal of Counseling and Development, 69,* 402–407.

Martin, J. (1991). To hypothesize or not to hypothesize. *American Psychologist, 46,* 651–652.

Martin, J. (1992). Cognitive-mediational research on counseling and psychotherapy. In S. G. Toukmanian & D. L. Rennie (Eds.), *Psychotherapy process research: Paradigmatic and narrative approaches* (pp. 108–133). Newbury Park, CA: Sage.

Martin, J., Cummings, A. L., & Hallberg, E. T. (1992). Therapists' intentional use of metaphor: Memorability, clinical impact, and possible epistemic/

motivational functions. *Journal of Consulting and Clinical Psychology, 60,* 143–145.

Martin, J., Paivio, S., & Labadie, D. (1990). Memory-enhancing characteristics of client-recalled important events in cognitive and experiential therapy: Integrating cognitive experimental and therapeutic psychology. *Counselling Psychology Quarterly, 3,* 239–256.

Martin, J., & Reaume, D. (1988). Cognitive structures of clients and counselors over time in therapy. Unpublished research data.

Martin, J., & Stelmaczonek, K. (1988). Participants' identification and recall of important events in counseling. *Journal of Counseling Psychology, 35,* 385–390.

McAdams, D. (1985). *Power, intimacy, and the life story.* Homewood, IL: Dorsey Press.

McMullen, L. M. (1985). Methods for studying the use of novel figurative language in psychotherapy. *Psychotherapy, 22,* 610–619.

McMullen, L. M. (1989). Use of figurative language in successful and unsuccessful cases of psychotherapy: Three comparisons. *Metaphor and Symbolic Activity, 4,* 203–225.

Mead, G. H. (1974). *Mind, self, and society.* Chicago: University of Chicago Press. (Original work published 1934)

Meichenbaum, D. (1977). *Cognitive-behavior modification: An integrative approach.* New York: Plenum.

Meichenbaum, D., & Jarmenko, M. E. (Eds.). (1983). *Stress reduction and prevention.* New York: Plenum.

Mendelson, J. (1979). The Habermas–Gadamer debate. *New German Critique, 18,* 3–26.

Mendler, J. M. (1984). *Stories, scripts, and scenes: Aspects of schema theory.* Hillsdale, NJ: Erlbaum.

Merleau-Ponty, M. (1945). *La phénoménologie de la perception.* Paris: Gallimard.

Middleton, D., & Edwards, D. (Eds.). (1990). *Collective remembering.* Newbury Park, CA: Sage.

Minsky, M. A. (1975). A framework for representing knowledge. In P. H. Winston (Ed.), *The psychology of computer vision* (pp. 211–217). New York: McGraw-Hill.

Much, N. C. (1992). The analysis of discourse as methodology for a semiotic psychology. *American Behavioral Scientist, 36,* 52–72.

Muran, J. C., & DiGiuseppi, R. A. (1990). Towards a cognitive formulation of metaphor use in psychotherapy. *Clinical Psychology Review, 10,* 69–85.

Neimeyer, R. A. (1986). Personal construct therapy. In W. Dryden & W. Golden (Eds.), *Cognitive-behavioral approaches to psychotherapy* (pp. 225–260). London: Harper & Row.

Neisser, U. (1976). *Cognition and reality.* San Francisco: Freeman.

Oyserman, D., & Markus, H. R. (1990). Possible selves and delinquency. *Journal of Personality and Social Psychology, 59,* 112–125.

Pace, T. M. (1988). Schema theory: A framework for research and practice in psychotherapy. *Journal of Cognitive Psychotherapy, 2,* 147–164.

Paivio, A. (1971). *Imagery and verbal processes.* New York: Holt, Rinehart and Winston.

Paivio, A. (1986). *Mental representations: A dual coding approach.* New York: Oxford University Press.

Paivio, S. (1989). *Action-act sequences in important therapeutic events: A case study of experiential psychotherapy.* Unpublished master's thesis, University of Western Ontario, London, Ontario.

Pedersen, P. B. (Ed.). (1991). Multiculturalism as a fourth force in counseling [Special issue]. *Journal of Counseling and Development, 70*(1), 1–250.

Pezdek, K., Whetstone, T., Reynolds, K., Askari, N., & Dougherty, T. (1989). Memory for real-world scenes: The role of consistency with schema expectation. *Journal of Experimental Psychology: Learning, Memory, and Cognition, 15,* 587–595.

Phillips, D. C. (1987). *Philosophy, science, and social inquiry: Contemporary methodological controversies in social science and related applied fields of research.* New York: Pergamon.

Piaget, J. (1969). *Judgment and reasoning in the child.* London: Routledge & Kegan Paul.

Polkinghorne, D. P. (1988). *Narrative psychology.* Albany: State University of New York Press.

Polkinghorne, D. P. (1991). Two conflicting calls for methodological reform. *The Counseling Psychologist, 19,* 103–114.

Pollio, H. R., & Barlow, J. M. (1975). A behavioral analysis of figurative language in psychotherapy: One session in a single case study. *Language and Speech, 18,* 236–254.

Popper, K. R. (1962). *Conjectures and refutations: The growth of scientific knowledge.* New York: Basic.

Popper, K. R. (1972). *Objective knowledge: An evolutionary approach.* Oxford: Clarendon.

Popper, K. R., & Eccles, J. C. (1977). *The self and its brain.* New York: Springer International.

Price, A., & Bucci, W. (1989). *The use of language in psychoanalysis and experiential psychotherapy.* Unpublished manuscript, Derner Institute for Advanced Psychological Studies, Adelphi University, Garden City, NY.

Proust, M. (1924). *Remembrance of things past.* New York: Random House.

Rice, L. N., & Greenberg, L. S. (Eds.). (1984). *Patterns of change: Intensive analysis of psychotherapy process.* New York: Guilford.

Rice, L. N., & Saperia, E. P. (1984). Task analysis of the resolution of problematic reactions. In L. N. Rice & L. S. Greenberg (Eds.), *Patterns of change: Intensive analysis of psychotherapy process* (pp. 29–66). New York: Guilford.

Rogers, C. R., Gendlin, G. T., Kiesler, D. J., & Truax, L. B. (1967). *The therapeutic relationship and its impact: A study of psychotherapy with schizophrenics.* Madison: University of Wisconsin Press.

Rorty, R. (1991a). Freud and moral reflection. In R. Rorty, *Essays on Heidegger and others: Philosophical papers* (Vol. 2; pp. 143–163). New York: Cambridge University Press.

Rorty, R. (1991b). Inquiry as recontextualization: An anti-dualist account of interpretation. In D. R. Hiley, J. F. Bohman, & R. Shusterman (Eds.), *The interpretive turn: Philosophy, science, culture* (pp. 59–80). Ithaca, NY: Cornell University Press.

Rosen, S. (1982). *My voice will go with you: The teaching tales of Milton H. Erickson.* New York: Norton.

Rummelhart, D. E. (1975). Notes on a schema for stories. In D. G. Bobrow & A. Collins (Eds.), *Representation and understanding: Studies in cognitive science* (pp. 211–236). New York: Academic.

Rummelhart, D. E., & Norman, D. A. (1981). Analogical processes in learning. In J. R. Anderson (Ed.), *Cognitive skills and their acquisition* (pp. 335–359). Hillsdale, NJ: Erlbaum.

Russell, R. L., & Van den Broek, P. (1992). Changing narrative schemas in psychotherapy. *Psychotherapy, 29,* 344–354.

Ryle, G. (1949). *The concept of mind.* London: Hutchinson.

Safran, J. D., Greenberg, L. S., & Rice, L. N. (1988). Integrating psychotherapy research and practice: Modeling the change process. *Psychotherapy, 25,* 1–17.

Sarbin, T. R. (Ed.). (1986). *Narrative psychology: The storied nature of human conduct.* New York: Praeger.

Schank, R., & Abelson, R. (1977). *Scripts, plans, goals, and understanding.* Hillsdale, NJ: Erlbaum.

Shepard, R. N. (1984). Ecological constraints on internal representation: Resonant kinematics of perceiving, imagining, thinking, and dreaming. *Psychological Review, 91,* 417–447.

Smedslund, J. (1979). Between the analytic and the arbitrary: A case study of psychological research. *Scandinavian Journal of Psychology, 20,* 129–140.

Smith, E. M. J., & Vasquez, M. J. T. (Eds.). (1985). Cross-cultural counseling [special issue]. *The Counseling Psychologist, 13*(4), 531–684.

Smith, M. L., & Glass, G. V. (1977). Meta-analysis of psychotherapy outcome studies. *American Psychologist, 32,* 752–760.

Smith, M. L., Glass, G. V., & Miller, T. I. (1980). *The benefits of psychotherapy.* Baltimore, MD: Johns Hopkins University Press.

Spence, D. P. (1984). *Narrative truth and historical truth.* New York: Norton.

Stiles, W. B., Shapiro, D. A., & Elliott, R. (1986). Are all therapies equivalent? *American Psychologist, 42,* 165–180.

Stiles, W. B., & Snow, J. S. (1984). Counseling session impact as viewed by novice counselors and their clients. *Journal of Counseling Psychology, 31,* 3–12.

Strong, S. R., & Claiborn, C. D. (1982). *Change through interaction: Social psychological processes of counseling and psychotherapy.* New York: Wiley.

Strong, S. R., Welsh, J. A., Corcoran, J. L., & Hoyt, W. T. (1992). Social psychology and counseling psychology: The history, products, and promise of an interface. *Journal of Counseling Psychology, 39,* 139–157.

Sugarman, J. (1992). *Reconceptualizing psychology: Subject-related phenomena in a quadrapartite space.* Unpublished manuscript, Simon Fraser University, Faculty of Education, Burnaby, BC, Canada.

Taylor, C. (1989). *Sources of the self.* Cambridge, MA: Harvard University Press.

Taylor, C. (1991). The dialogical self. In D. R. Hiley, J. F. Bohman, & R. Shusterman (Eds.), *The interpretive turn: Philosophy, science, culture* (pp. 304–314). Ithaca, NY: Cornell University Press.

Taylor, C. (1992). *Multiculturalism and "the politics of recognition": An essay by Charles Taylor.* Princeton, NJ: Princeton University Press.

Toukmanian, S. G. (1986). A measure of client perceptual processing. In L. S. Greenberg & W. M. Pinsof (Eds.), *The psychotherapeutic process: A research handbook* (pp. 107–130). New York: Guilford.

Toukmanian, S. G. (1992). Studying the client's perceptual processes and their outcomes in psychotherapy. In S. G. Toukmanian & D. L. Rennie (Eds.), *Psychotherapy process research: Paradigmatic and narrative approaches* (pp. 77–107). Newbury Park, CA: Sage.

Tulving, E. (1983). *Elements of episodic memory.* New York: Oxford University Press.

Tulving, E. (1985). How many memory systems are there? *American Psychologist, 40,* 385–398.

Tulving, E., Schacter, D. L., & Stark, H. (1982). Priming effects in word-fragment completion are independent of recognition memory. *Journal of Experimental Psychology: Human Learning and Memory, 8,* 336–342.

Turk, D. C., & Salovey, P. (1985). Cognitive structures, cognitive processes, and cognitive-behavioral modification: I. Client issues. *Cognitive Therapy and Research, 9,* 1–17.

Vygotsky, L. (1981). The genesis of higher mental functions. In J. V. Wertsch (Ed.), *The concept of activity in Soviet psychology* (pp. 160–166). Armonk, NY: M. E. Sharpe.

Vygotsky, L. (1986). *Thought and language.* Cambridge, MA: MIT Press. (Original work published 1934)

Watzlawick, P. (1978). *The language of change.* New York: Basic.

Wertsch, J. V. (1991). *Voices of the mind: A sociocultural approach to mediated action.* New York: Cambridge University Press.

Wexler, D. A., & Rice, L. N. (Eds.). (1974). *Innovations in client-centered therapy.* New York: Wiley–Interscience.

Widdershoven, G. A. M. (1992). Hermeneutics and relativism: Wittgenstein, Gadamer, Habermas. *Theoretical and Philosophical Psychology, 12,* 1–11.

Wittgenstein, L. (1953). *Philosophical investigations.* Oxford: Blackwell.

Wood, F., Ebert, V., & Kinsbourne, M. (1982). The episodic-semantic distinction in memory and amnesia: Clinical and experimental observations. In L. S. Cermak (Ed.), *Human memory and amnesia* (pp. 167–193). Hillsdale, NJ: Erlbaum.

Yesenosky, J. M., & Dowd, E. T. (1990). The social psychology of counselling and psychotherapy: A base for integration. *British Journal of Guidance and Counselling, 18,* 170–184.

Zimring, F. M. (1974). Theory and practice of client-centered therapy: A cognitive view. In D. A. Wexler & L. N. Rice (Eds.), *Innovations in client-centered therapy.* New York: Wiley–Interscience.

Index

133

ABOUT THE AUTHOR

Since receiving his Ph.D. from the University of Alberta in 1973, **Jack Martin** has held Faculty positions in education and psychology at the University of Alberta, Deakin University (Australia), the University of Western Ontario, the University of Iowa, and Simon Fraser University where he currently is Professor of Counseling and Educational Psychology. He is a Fellow of the American Psychological Association through the Divisions of Counseling Psychology, Psychotherapy, and Theoretical/Philosophical Psychology. He is a past recipient of the award for research in counseling and human development given by the American Educational Research Association. He has just completed a three year term as Research Editor for the *Journal of Counseling and Development*, and is currently a Consulting Editor for the *Journal of Counseling Psychology*. He also is co-author, with Lisa T. Hoshmand, of a forthcoming book, also to be published by Teachers College Press, tentatively titled, *Method Choice and Inquiry Process: Lessons from Programmatic Research on Psychotherapy Practice*.